THE QUEST FOR HAPPINESS

THE QUEST FOR HAPPINESS

THE INNER PATH TO TRUE FULFILMENT

The Divine Discourses of

NIRYAPAK MUNI
SHREE VEER SAGAR JI

Compiled and written by
Jyoti Jain Tholiya

AMARYLLIS

AMARYLLIS

An imprint of Manjul Publishing House Pvt. Ltd.
• C-16, Sector 3, Noida, Uttar Pradesh 201301, India
Website: www.manjulindia.com

Registered Office:
• 2nd Floor, Usha Preet Complex, 42 Malviya Nagar,
Bhopal 462 003 – India

Distribution Centres
Ahmedabad, Bengaluru, Chennai, Hyderabad,
Kochi, Kolkata, Mumbai, Noida, Pune

The Quest for Happiness: The Inner Path to True Fulfilment
by Jyoti Jain Tholiya

This edition published in paperback by
Amaryllis, an imprint of Manjul Publishing House Pvt. Ltd. in 2025

ISBN 978-81-981844-0-5

Cover design: Wasim Helal

Printed and bound in India by Replika Press Private Limited.

Dedicated to Niryapak Muni Shree Veer Sagar Ji,
whose teachings and blessings made this book possible

CONTENTS

Part 4
Communication and Relationships

Part 5
Personal Growth and Resilience

Part 6
Cultivating Gratitude and Reflection

PREFACE

Niryapak Muni Shree Veer Sagar Ji conducted the *'Sukh ki Khoj'* (The Quest for Happiness) series during chaturmas 2023 in Pune. The sole purpose of these sessions was to explore how we can transform our lives. Inspired by Gurudev's teachings, I felt compelled to compile this book from his insightful pravachan series, illuminating the path to genuine fulfilment.

In a world where the pursuit of happiness often feels like an endless quest, we must recognise that true happiness is not merely the absence of sadness or the pursuit of material success. It is a complex, multifaceted experience, deeply rooted in emotional well-being, meaningful relationships, and a strong sense of purpose. This book aims to guide you toward discovering true happiness—one that transcends superficial joy.

The book is divided into six parts, comprising twenty-five chapters. Each chapter includes **Actionables** to help you internalise and apply what you have learned. This section focuses on how well you understand and implement these lessons in your life. Imagine viewing the individuals in the stories you will come across as reflections of your own experiences. Consider how you would respond in similar situations. This reflective approach will help you apply the lessons learned to your own life. Be honest in your self-assessment, so that when writing your answers, you can gain the most benefit.

We begin with **Understanding Happiness**, where we define what real happiness means, explore its diverse sources, and acknowledge the essential roles of happiness and sadness. This foundational section teaches us that real happiness is never found outside of us; it lies within us.

Next, we delve into **Mindfulness and Acceptance**. Here, you will discover how cultivating mindfulness can enhance your awareness and emotional regulation, enabling you to embrace the present more completely. Acceptance is a crucial aspect of this journey, offering practical strategies for managing expectations and embracing life as it is. You can cultivate a deeper sense of peace by embracing acceptance through mindfulness and meditation.

In **Overcoming Barriers**, we address common obstacles that hinder our happiness. From the traps of overthinking and unnecessary thoughts, to the challenges posed by jealousy and attachment, this section provides actionable strategies to break free from these constraints and strengthen emotional resilience.

As we transition into **Communication and Relationships**, we explore the vital role of effective communication in our connections with others. By mastering nonviolent communication and nurturing healthy relationships, we can create environments that support our happiness and uplift those around us, especially within the dynamics of family, where love and support can either uplift or drain our spirits.

In **Personal Growth and Resilience**, we encourage you to step outside your comfort zone, confront fears, and develop practical tools to manage anxiety. Embracing discomfort is essential for growth, and through this exploration, you will find that true liberation often lies just beyond familiar boundaries.

Finally, in **Cultivating Gratitude and Reflection**, we highlight the transformative power of gratitude and the importance of self-analysis. By reflecting on our experiences and learning to let go, we open ourselves to new possibilities and a deeper sense of happiness.

This book is not merely a guide to be followed; it is an invitation to embark on a transformative journey together. This book aims to deepen your understanding of real happiness and empower you to find your own path.

May your journey lead you to a life filled with joy, peace, and meaningful connections. Welcome to *The Quest for Happiness*!

Dr Jyoti Jain Tholiya

PART 1

UNDERSTANDING HAPPINESS

WHAT IS REAL HAPPINESS?

Everyone desires happiness, but how many can truly say they have found it? Have you ever asked yourself why you do the things you do each day? Most of the time, behind every goal you set or decision you make—whether it is relocating to a new city, choosing a career path, or buying something—there is one common reason: you want to be happy. But what exactly is real happiness? Everyone talks about it, chases it, and dreams of it, yet very few people truly understand what it means or how to achieve it. This book invites you to slow down and reflect: Am I truly happy, or simply striving to be? Before we explore the major decisions that shape our lives, let us begin by uncovering what happiness really means—and why it matters more than we often realise.

Migration theories, for example, often emphasise the relationship between happiness and material well-being. At their core, these theories suggest that people move—

especially to metro cities—not just in search of jobs, education, or a better lifestyle, but ultimately, in search of happiness. Most of you have migrated with this very hope: to find a more fulfilling life. But this is where things become complex.

The idea of happiness is not universal. People from different backgrounds and cultures emphasise on the different aspects of this transient state. Some see happiness as inner peace and satisfaction with their surroundings and achievements, while others find it in engaging careers and exciting hobbies. But is there a single, clear definition of happiness, or is it somewhat ambiguous for most people? What is your take on this?

In psychology, a prominent theoretical framework known as the four stages of competence explains the cognitive progression individuals undergo when acquiring proficiency in a novel skill or domain of knowledge. The concept consists of four stages: a) unconscious incompetence, b) conscious incompetence, c) conscious competence, and d) unconscious competence.

The first stage—unconscious incompetence—means, 'I don't know what I don't know.' This is a state marked by unawareness and complete ignorance. Individuals neither understand, nor possess the ability to execute the task at hand, often failing to address this knowledge deficit. The second stage—conscious incompetence—means, 'I know what I don't know.' Here, individuals are aware and recognise and address the identified deficiency. The third stage—conscious competence—denotes, 'I know what I know.' Individuals comprehend the skill or knowledge and demonstrate the capability to perform it conscientiously. The fourth stage is unconscious competence, where individuals have self-mastered their skill to a degree that its execution becomes nearly automatic and second nature to them, with minimal conscious effort required.

Now, imagine the quest for happiness as a journey through these four stages. People in the first stage don't even think of happiness. Like small children; they're completely ignorant of the concept. In the second stage, people are a bit wiser and realise that happiness is missing from their lives. In third stage, they actively start pursuing happiness and are on the path to finding it. Finally, in the last stage, they achieve true happiness by going through extreme conditions. Most people fall into the second category, as they struggle to find happiness despite working hard for it.

However, in today's world, it seems that the true meaning of happiness is lost. It is important to understand what real happiness is and to clearly define what you want in life. Happiness is not merely achieving goals—because after achieving the goal, one must become happy and content. But are you happy after achieving your goal of eating your favourite food, buying a new flat, or being blessed with a son, daughter, wife, or husband? Perhaps not.

One person seeks happiness in living with loved ones while another finds it in earning money. However, if the loved ones pass away, or if the money is lost or stolen, happiness goes away instantly. This is fleeting happiness. So, true happiness is not a state to arrive at, which goes away after a while and then you have to seek something else. It is not something you need to constantly chase.

In the present world, it is evident that many people are constantly striving for more and more. Almost everyone is suffering from depression, anxiety, and mental stress these days. One of the most prominent reasons is that individual happiness and well-being are now directly influenced by money or material possessions. True happiness lies in maintaining a positive mindset, living a healthy lifestyle—and being free from worry, tension, and anxiety—regardless of the situation. Happiness is letting go of distress and being content with what you have. However, when you do not accept that internally, your mind is in denial mode.

Let us understand this better, through a short story that reflects how often we search for happiness outside ourselves, rather than within.

Long ago, an old lady was searching for something outside her hut on the street. Curious onlookers approached her and asked, 'What are you looking for?' The old lady replied, 'I dropped a needle.' People asked, 'Don't you remember in which part of the street the needle fell? It is getting dark, and soon there won't be enough light to search.' She calmly responded, 'I didn't drop it out here—I dropped it inside my house.' Surprised, they asked, 'Then why are you looking for it outside?'

The old lady's actions teach us a profound lesson: we often search externally for what is actually missing internally. The moral of the story is: do not seek happiness outside yourself; it hasn't been lost anywhere. While you spend your life searching for it externally, happiness has been present within you all this while.

Much like the old lady in the story, we often overlook the fact that true happiness stems from within ourselves. It is a state of mind rooted in contentment and mindfulness, not dependent on external factors such as wealth, social status or approval, and material possessions. By cultivating gratitude for what we have and making conscious choices, we can achieve a deep sense of happiness that is independent of our circumstances. Ultimately, the most meaningful measure of success, lies in the level of happiness we experience consistently; highlighting the profound connection between our inner selves and our overall well-being.

Actionables

- Evaluate your current level of happiness on a scale from zero to ten, where zero signifies the worst and ten indicates the best.
- Reflect on which stage of competence you are in.
- Mull over whether happiness is simply a state that arises when your wishes are fulfilled.
- Write down the key factors that influence your happiness.

Reminders:

- Real happiness is never found outside of us; it lies within us.
- Happiness is not dependent; it is independent.
- True happiness is not a fleeting state of mind to arrive at.
- Happiness is a consistent feeling, not a temporary one.

THINGS IN WHICH WE SEEK HAPPINESS

EVERYONE YEARNS FOR HAPPINESS IN LIFE, YET IT OFTEN remains elusive. Instead of finding happiness, they encounter sorrow. People seek happiness in various external sources—whether in relationship, possessions, physical well-being, or the fleeting emotions within our minds. Analogous to a deer relentlessly searching for the fragrance of musk in the entire forest—oblivious to the fact that it resides in its own navel—worldly individuals persistently search for happiness externally. In various aspects of life, you may believe that accumulating more will lead to greater happiness, but the ultimate question remains: does continuous accumulation truly bring happiness?

People hold diverse beliefs about what constitutes happiness. Some find joy in eating, drinking, dressing well, travelling, or enjoying a certain lifestyle. But this raises a question: what emotions do you actually experience after satisfying your needs or desires? In practical terms, the process often involves desiring something, fulfilling that desire, and subsequently experiencing a sense of happiness. For instance, when we feel hungry, our body craves nourishment to alleviate the discomfort. Eating food gradually eases the pain of hunger. Similarly, quenching thirst with water, brings a sense of relief and joy by relieving the discomfort of thirst.

This leads us to a deeper question: is it the alleviation of pain that we refer to as happiness, or is it something different altogether? Consider this. What would you prefer: the absence of pain from the beginning, or the experience of pain followed by its relief which we associate with happiness? Regardless of how you define happiness, it is ultimately rooted in some expectation or desire.

Consider the experience of eating ice cream or your favourite sweet. Immerse yourself in the moment by observing the entire process with mindfulness, and notice how long the sensation of happiness actually persists. Upon consuming the ice cream, an immediate sense of joy arises. However, examine how long this happiness endures—does it last while it is on your tongue, during the chewing process, while swallowing, or until it reaches your stomach? What transpires afterward? It is quite possible that once the ice cream is finished, a desire for more arises, and your mental state begins to fluctuate. How did that initial feeling emerge? Did it arise solely from the ice cream, or did it originate within you? The critical question is: where does happiness truly come from?

If the taste of ice cream remains consistent from beginning to end, then logically, the pleasure it brings should remain the same as well. However, there is often variation in your feelings. Throughout the entire process of consuming it, your emotions shift; implying that the source of happiness is not inherent in the ice cream but rather within you. The happiness derived from ice cream is merely a temporary relief from discomfort or craving. What is commonly referred to as happiness through external objects is, in essence, not lasting joy. Seeking happiness outside ourselves provides only temporary satisfaction; it lacks permanence. True happiness is that which is born gradually within and endures forever.

It is important to distinguish, between the relief of physical discomfort and the broader concept of happiness.

For instance, if you have a fever of 105 degrees F, taking medicine that lowers your temperature to 101 degrees F may not necessarily bring a feeling of happiness, per se. Instead, the drop in temperature is more likely to bring relief from the discomfort or distress caused by high fever. As the temperature further decreases to 98 degrees F, the sense of improvement is primarily due to the diminishing physical discomfort. The improved state you experience in such a case is better understood as relief from physical distress, rather than true happiness in the conventional sense.

Happiness, in a broader emotional and psychological context, is a complex and multifaceted experience—one that encompasses far more than just physical well-being.

The thermometer serves as an instrument to measure temperature, much like ice cream acts as a medium, to evoke a particular feeling within us. Similarly, various things in life are crafted or used as mediums through which we seek external happiness. Whether it is food, clothing, air conditioning, a car, or a house, our emotions often arise from the absence of the desired thing. When we plan for and attain the desired object, we relieve the discomfort or sadness associated with its absence—a state we then label as happiness. This perspective suggests that what we often term as happiness, is actually the reduction of the discomfort or dissatisfaction linked to unfulfilled desires.

The sources from which we seek happiness in life are categorised into four distinct groups. The first category involves non-living objects, as many people tend to accumulate possessions. The second category encompasses living beings, while the third pertains to aspects related to our own bodies. The fourth category focuses on the emotions that arise within our minds.

By understanding and contemplating these four categories, many concepts associated with happiness can become clearer. This approach offers a new perspective on how we perceive the world, pursue happiness, and engage in the quest for fulfilment. It holds the potential to bring about significant changes in our attitudes and behaviours. Although we live in this world and interact with it daily, exploring these dimensions may prove to be a novel and eye-opening experience—prompting a re-evaluation of our beliefs and actions.

It is essential, to periodically review the desires that linger in our minds, and evaluate them against the backdrop of our limited lifespan. This introspective evaluation—prompts us to reflect on the feasibility of our goals, and question the direction in which we are heading. The key lies in adapting our perspectives, revising our viewpoints, and acknowledging the realities of our circumstances. Without such shifts, achieving genuine happiness may remain elusive. We stand a better chance of creating a fulfilling and meaningful life, by acknowledging the impermanence of desires, and aligning our pursuits, with both our evolving aspirations and constraints we face.

Actionables

Fill in the below matrix. What are the things or objects, whether they fulfil your needs or desires, that bring you happiness, and which are the ones that bring you sadness?

From	Needs		Wants/Desires	
	Happiness	Sadness	Happiness	Sadness
Non-living beings				
Living beings				
Our own body				
Our own emotions				

Reminders:

- Seeking happiness in external objects provides only temporary satisfaction; it lacks permanence.
- True happiness is that which is born once and endures forever.

EMOTIONS OF HAPPINESS AND SADNESS

UNDERSTANDING THE SPECIFIC EMOTIONS THAT CAUSE distress is essential, and the origins of this emotional pain often trace back to external influences. Our primary emotional experiences, whether joy or sadness, hold significant importance. External factors, separate from ourselves, often trigger these emotions. People, objects, or situations merely act as a conduit not source, of our emotional states. It is important to explore why unhappiness tends to linger, while happiness often feels fleeting.

In today's materialistic world, distinguishing between non-living and living entities is relatively easy—they are visible and tangible. But grasping the intangible—our inner emotional world—is far more challenging. Identifying which emotions lead to happiness and which give rise to sadness, prompts meaningful reflection. Yet, we often neglect the internal consequences of these emotions that incessantly trouble us, and those that internally uplift us with joy. It is therefore imperative to undertake a more mindful assessment of our emotions.

Emotions can be broadly categorised into two types: positive emotions that bring forth feelings of happiness, and negative emotions that, when internalised, lead to feelings of sadness. Understanding the distinction between these emotional states, is crucial for cultivating a more fulfilling and content life.

To deepen this understanding, let us examine the four primary कषाय *(kashayas)* or passions, namely: क्रोध *(krodha)* or anger, मान *(maan)* or ego, माया *(maya)* or deceit, लोभ *(lobha)* or greed. In Jain philosophy, kashayas refers to deep-seated emotional tendencies—anger, ego, deceit, and greed—that bind the soul to the cycle of karma and worldly existence. Here, anger and ego fall under the broader category of hatred, while deceit and greed are considered forms of attachments or reactions that cloud right perception, hinder spiritual progress and perpetuate karmic bondage.

Now let us explore the origin and fundamental causes behind our desires. The journey often commences with our greed and aspirations. Nothing materialises without some form of greed. Without greed, desires cannot even take root. In any given scenario, if we scrutinise it closely, it invariably starts with a form of greed. A desire emerges within us, and individuals might resort to deceit to fulfil that desire. Upon achieving their goal through such means, they experience temporary satisfaction. Following this satisfaction, the focus shifts to the ego. This individual now begins to feel a sense of superiority and accomplishment.

Consider the act of deceiving someone; does it bring about joy or sorrow? Initially, it may bring a fleeting sense of satisfaction, which can be mistaken for happiness. However, this satisfaction eventually transforms into the cause of ego, ultimately leading to sadness. The nuance lies in recognising this subtle difference, as failing to understand it can lead to confusion; misinterpreting the source of sadness as happiness and vice versa.

According to Jain scriptures, ego is classified into eight distinct types: the ego of knowledge, worship, family, lineage, power/strength, superhuman attainment, austerity, and the body. The ego arises when we accomplish what we have desired or when we obtain something effortlessly. The moment something becomes an accomplishment, the ego begins to manifest.

The emotions triggered by the four kashayas can lead to both happiness and sadness. While anger typically results in sorrow, paradoxically, some individuals may feel a momentary satisfaction in expressing it. Yet, it is important to understand that genuine joy is absent in such moments. Anger, in particular, is detrimental to both mental and physical health. Modern medical research has confirmed its harmful impact on emotional well-being and its connection to various physical health issues.

A team of doctors conducted an insightful study involving eight participants, divided into two groups of four. The first group was instructed to focus on their enemies. For thirty minutes, they were asked to reflect on the worst aspects of their enemies, writing down their names, and expressing their anger in the most intense manner possible. Blood samples were taken from all four participants before and after this exercise. Additionally, they were given an outlet to vent their anger. Upon analysing the blood reports, the doctors were surprised to find a significant decrease in the counts of White Blood Cells (WBC) and Red Blood Cells (RBC), indicating a notable negative impact on the participants' immune system and overall health.

In contrast, the second group was instructed to focus on positive emotions. They were instructed to think about friends who exuded kindness, and compassion, and helpfulness. The participants were given thirty minutes to engage in this reflective exercise, and blood samples were taken before and after. The results were astonishing once again, but in a positive direction. The WBC and RBC counts showed a significant increase, suggesting a positive effect on both immune function and overall health.

This research highlights the profound influence of emotions, both negative and positive on physiological well-being, further highlighting the intricate connection between mental and physical health. The conclusion drawn from the research was significant. It highlighted that individuals worldwide harbour feelings of anger, resentment, and unfulfilled desires, often dwelling on negative thoughts about others. The medical findings revealed that individuals who consistently bear harmful thoughts, experience a significant reduction in the levels of RBC and WBC in their blood. On the contrary, those individuals who cultivate positive feelings, exhibit kindness, and harbour good intentions towards others, demonstrate an automatic physiological response leading to improved health. This suggests, that maintaining a positive and compassionate mindset contributes to overall well-being and resilience.

At the core of our emotional experience lies the secretion of specific neurochemicals, primarily oxytocin and dopamine. For instance, feelings of love trigger the release of oxytocin, often called the love hormone, which contributes to a sense of emotional warmth and trust. On the contrary, anger and aggressive behaviour can lead to the release of dopamine, potentially causing internal harm by damaging cells. Moreover, excessive cravings and the compulsive urge to acquire material possessions can also stimulate the release of dopamine. Conversely, acts of generosity and the desire to give trigger the release of oxytocin, promoting happiness and emotional well-being. This interconnected relationship between emotions and biochemical responses accentuates the impact of our emotional states, on both our mental and physical well-being.

Positive emotions trigger the release of oxytocin, while negative emotions stimulate the release of dopamine. An analogy can be drawn to the agricultural practice—where cows and buffaloes are injected with oxytocin to increase milk production. Similarly, within our bodies, affection and positive emotions elevate oxytocin levels. As the quantity of oxytocin rises, feelings of love and goodwill expand, leading to a natural inclination toward sharing. Acts of generosity, giving, helping, or serving others further stimulate the release of oxytocin, deepening our experience of joy and contentment. This interconnected relationship highlights the profound impact of positive emotions on our overall well-being.

Conversely, negative emotions such as excessive sadness, greed, and fear can trigger the release of dopamine. Research indicates that when an individual's dopamine levels surge excessively, it can lead to a downward spiral toward depression. Excessive greed, acting as a catalyst for dopamine secretion, has also been linked to detrimental mental states. In instances where anger, greed, and fear coalesce, causing an overproduction of dopamine, the individual is propelled towards a cascade of negativity and diminished well-being.

Now, categorise individuals based on their emotional tendencies, and you will find a distinction between those who embody positive qualities and those who exhibit negative traits. This differentiation extends to emotions like constructive anger versus destructive anger, as well as beneficial versus detrimental attachment. When we transcend our physical appearances and genuinely empathise with others, we cultivate a sense of benevolence—a heartfelt desire for their well-being. This includes the wish for others to be free from suffering, poverty, and misfortune. In this context, even greed can take a positive form—a selfless desire for the happiness and welfare of others. Similarly, attachment to a higher purpose, such as devotion to God and or reverence for a guru, is considered a positive form of attachment, one that brings happiness. Now imagine a world devoid of deception and illusion, where pride and anger have no place. In such a realm, pure, virtuous, and unblemished love that transcends negative emotions and embodies true goodness, prevails.

Now consider anger—is it a cause or an effect? In truth, anger functions as both cause and effect. Think about a time when you were stuck in traffic on your way to an important meeting. You felt frustrated because your desire to be on time was not being met—that is anger as an effect. But then, because you were still angry, you might have spoken harshly to a coworker when you got to work, which caused tension for the rest of the day—that is, anger acting as a cause. If we do not deal with it, anger like this can build up stress, create conflicts with others, and even harm our health over time. That is why it is so important to understand where these emotions come from. They do not just bother us in the moment—they can shape how we think, act, and feel long into the future.

Emotions that merely provide external gratification often fail to nourish our inner well-being. Once this concept is comprehended, we can discern and manage these emotions effectively. It is essential to introspect—which emotions lead us toward sorrow, and which ones bring genuine joy? We must ask ourselves—where is our anger, ego, deceit, and greed taking us? A conscious effort to observe, question, and transform these emotional patterns is fundamental to long-term peace and well-being.

Actionables

Fill in the below matrix. Which emotions bring us happiness and which emotions cause us sadness?

Our own emotions	Happiness	Sadness
Greed		
Deceit		
Ego		
Anger		
Jealousy		
Stress		

Reminders:

- Anger and ego stem from hatred, while deceit and greed arise from attachment and possessive desire.
- We must ask ourselves: where is our anger, ego, deceit, and greed leading us? Gaining insight into these emotional patterns—and consciously addressing them—is essential for lasting well-being.

PART 2

MINDFULNESS AND ACCEPTANCE

MINDFULNESS

OUR MIND IS THE KEY TO BOTH HAPPINESS AND sorrow. It is crucial to have a peaceful and stable mind for true happiness. In nature, animals live freely and joyfully without tension or worry, content with very little. In contrast, despite having homes, wealth, status, and social circles, many people today often seem troubled. Animals, with the same senses and basic needs as humans find joy in simplicity, while we often become more troubled as we accumulate more. Possessions and attachments, instead of bringing peace, frequently add to our anxiety. Think about our grandparents' generation—they lived without many of the amenities we consider essential today: air conditioning, cars, mobile phones, or computers. Yet, wasn't their life more content and less complicated? As modern conveniences have increased, happiness has paradoxically decreased. This suggests that growing greed, and expanding needs may blur our understanding of true contentment.

How, then, can we attain lasting happiness and rise above sorrow? Mindfulness offers a way forward. It is the state of effortless alertness—but achieving this effortless state requires a unique effort. Only with such inner discipline can one truly transcend the world while still living within it, like a lotus that remains above the water. Mindfulness, achieved through consistent and dedicated effort, allows a person to live in a higher state of awareness, balance, and peace.

A powerful technique to rise above the chaos of daily life is to practice complete mindfulness—being fully alert and present in each moment. Try to perceive things in their true form, without the distortions of ego or pre-conceived notions. This approach can lead to a profound shift, in how we experience and interact with the world.

True peace and insight arise, when we shift from ego toward a state of devotion and humility. In Hindi, the word मनन *(manan)* refers to contemplation, reflection, and thoughtful analysis. However, true manan begins where the mind's constant chatter ends—it is the stillness beyond thoughts. Another word, नमन *(naman)*, means bowing down, feeling gratitude, and being in complete devotion. The outcome of manan is naman. When one practices naman they rise above the mind's ego and its subtle arrogance, transitioning from sorrow to inner joy. This journey from manan to naman brings profound joy and unique inner experiences, guiding the mind in the right direction. When manan leads to naman, we become truly receptive to what life offers. To understand this more clearly, we must reflect on how we approach situations. Are we seeing things as they truly are, or are our perceptions clouded by mental noise and emotional filters? When we calm ourselves and approach situations with full alertness and mindfulness, everything begins to appear in a new light.

Real peace and happiness arise from a stable and focused mind. Many people seek happiness through the recitation of mantras, yet often, fail to find the fulfilment they desire. The true power of a mantra does not lie merely in its words, but in the state of mind with which it is recited. Acharya Shree Vidya Sagar Ji Maharaj has emphasised that the effectiveness of a mantra depends entirely on the stability of the mind. When the mind is calm and devoted, even the simplest words can become deeply powerful. It is this inner stillness and focus that transforms words into a source of spiritual energy.

A mantra is meant to guide the mind; beyond its words to a higher state of consciousness, much like how a child looks beyond the mother's pointing finger to see the moon. Focusing solely on the mantra's literal words, causes us to miss its true essence. The deeper teaching here is that neither mantras nor situations, are inherently good or bad rather, it is the state of our mind that determines how we perceive and use them.

A stable mind can harness the full potential of a mantra, while an unstable mind leads to distraction and confusion. Similarly, situations are not inherently good or bad; it is our perspective and how we approach them that shapes our experience. In the same way, mantras are not intrinsically powerful or ineffective; their impact depends on the clarity and steadiness of our minds. A clear and focused mind will find the good in any situation, and effectively tap into the power of a mantra, while a disturbed mind will focus on the negative and miss the true essence.

There was a king who was deeply troubled and distressed. He went to his guru and asked for a mantra that could bring him peace. The king confessed that his mind was full of sorrow and anxiety. The guru responded, 'I will give you a solution, but you must come back tomorrow morning and bring your troubled mind with you.' The condition was clear: the king had to bring his distressed state of mind, or no solution would be offered. That night, the king desperately tried to hold on to his troubled mind, knowing he had to present it to his guru. He could not sleep, preoccupied with preserving his sorrowful state. As soon as the clock struck 4 am, he arrived at the guru's ashram.

The guru asked, 'Where is your troubled mind?' The king replied, 'I don't know where it has gone.' The guru then said, 'This is the solution: as soon as you attempt to observe your troubled mind, it starts to calm down on its own. When we do not see it as it is, the distress increases. But when we observe it with full awareness, the feelings of distress begin to settle down by themselves.' This story illustrates that when we fully confront and observe our inner turmoil, rather than avoiding or ignoring it, the distress starts to dissolve, and we find peace.

Whenever you encounter significant problems in life, you should try to observe the situation from a 360-degree perspective, i.e., practice साक्षी भाव *(being aware)*. By simply observing reality as it is, without judgement or reaction, the mind begins to stabilise. This calmness reduces distress and opens pathways to solutions. Stress tends to block creative thinking, by triggering biochemical reactions that amplify suffering. However, when we practice mindfulness and adopt a witnessing state, our mind begins to function more productively, entering a more creative and solution-oriented phase.

Scientific evidence shows that staying calm and practicing mindfulness, can enhance mental function and creativity. This involves fully experiencing activities through your senses, and reflecting on your feelings. This practice helps you become more mindful, and prevents immediate reactions to life events. Instead, you will analyse situations first, leading to a more stable mind. Over time, this self-observation adopts a neutral mindset, allowing for constructive responses even in challenging situations.

Often, we accept what aligns with our pre-conceptions and biases, rather than objective truth. We tend to embrace what we believe or what aligns with our emotions and attachments, rather than what is true. We often interpret situations and people based on our personal perspectives and emotional attachments, rather than on an objective assessment of reality. The situation is perceived as we want to see it rather than how it actually is. We only see what we have set in our mindset, not what is truly there. Therefore, everything is influenced by our mind. We should try to view situations with complete alertness as they are, without any bias. By being neutral and observing, we begin to understand things differently and find solutions. Mindfulness has a profound impact, changing our perspective completely.

If you approach every experience with the witnessing state and an attitude of reverence, the true power of a mantra begins to unfold. Mantras, gurus, and scriptures are all mediums—tools meant to guide us towards a higher state of awareness. However, the ultimate goal is to reach the moon, not to get stuck on the finger pointing towards it. Yet, many people get stuck on the medium or on the words of mantras or the authority of the scriptures—rather than progressing toward the deeper truth they signify.

When life becomes challenging and problems feel overwhelming, it is helpful to view everything through the lens of true reality. This involves understanding and accepting things as they truly are, rather than through our own perceived reality. Often, we interpret situations and people based on our own biases and perceptions instead of recognising the actual truth. This leads us to misjudge situations, reacting not to what is truly happening but to our interpretation of it.

For example, if we hold a certain image of someone in our mind, our perception of their actions will be filtered through that image. Nathuram Godse perceived Mahatma Gandhi in a particular way, while the rest of the world saw him differently, and even Gandhi had his own self-perception. Similarly, when we form an image of someone, our reactions to their actions are influenced by that image. This concept emphasises that our understanding of reality, is frequently filtered through our own biases. By striving to see things as they truly are, without the distortions of our pre-conceptions, we can approach challenges and interactions with greater clarity, equanimity, and peace.

Immediate reactions without understanding often spiral out of control. Many people regret reacting in anger or saying things they did not truly mean. Developing a witnessing state—by practicing mindfulness even in simple acts like eating, seeing, sitting, or sleeping, even if just for a minute or two—can help you stay anchored. This consistent practice cultivates calmness, enhances self-awareness, and allows you to channel your energy more meaningfully toward personal growth.

Actionables

In your daily activities, practice observing things with all five senses in a neutral way. Then, observe your thoughts and feelings without labelling them as good or bad—just let them be. As you develop this practice, you will find yourself pausing, to analyse situations before reacting. This will help you approach situations more thoughtfully and calmly.

For example, when you eat something like gulab jamun, engage your senses and mind in the following way:

- **Touch:** Notice the texture of the gulab jamun. Is it soft or firm?
- **Smell:** Pay attention to its fragrance. What is it?
- **Sight:** Observe its appearance. Is it round, oval, or irregular? What colour is it?
- **Sound:** Listen carefully. Is there any sound associated with it, perhaps while being prepared or served?
- **Taste:** Take a bite and notice the taste. Is it sweet? Is it sweeter than you expected?

After observing these sensory details, turn your attention to your feelings about the gulab jamun. Are you enjoying it, feeling indifferent, or disliking it? Are you eating it out of desire or obligation?

Reminders:

- Real peace and happiness come from having a stable mind.
- Mantras themselves are neither good nor bad; it is a stable mind that makes a mantra effective.
- True peace and insight arise, when we shift from ego to a state of devotion and humility.
- Mindfulness achieved through consistent and dedicated effort, allows a person to live in a higher state of consciousness and peace.

HOW TO LIVE LIFE WITHOUT EXPECTATIONS?

EXPECTATIONS SIGNIFICANTLY INFLUENCE OUR happiness, often making us dependent on others, and giving them control over our emotions. Although, living completely without expectations is challenging, we can find a happier and more balanced life, by gradually reducing our expectations. The less we expect, the more control we have over ourselves—resulting in greater inner peace, happiness, and fewer emotional entanglements.

You may remain physically engaged, but inwardly connected to your true self. This balance is difficult, but possible, when we align our thoughts with this eternal truth and make the soul our primary focus. When we live this way, expectations no longer arise in the mind. By shifting our focus inward and prioritising our soul, we can reduce expectations and achieve contentment.

However, we also experience joy in family, society, friends, jobs, and money. How then, do we balance this? How do we stay connected to our centre without abandoning it, while also engaging with the periphery when necessary? The key lies in aligning our actions with our core values. Fulfil your duties and participate in social life, but always return to your centre. Returning to the centre, does not mean abandoning your responsibilities; it means staying inwardly connected while being outwardly engaged.

So, the question arises: if we remain at the centre, will our interactions fade away? Not at all. But when we constantly move around the periphery—seeking approval, reacting to others—we hand over the control of our emotions to the world. Countless people begin to influence our joy, anger, sorrow, and stress. To live without expectations, means keeping your remote control in your own hands, not in someone else's. We must understand that our happiness or sadness should not depend on others. Through self-realisation and self-control, we can live a happy and balanced life.

Why do we develop expectations from everyone? We develop expectations, because we believe we are doing something for others. Parents expect things from their children, wives from their husbands, husbands from their wives and children—and even from people outside the family. This sense of 'I am doing,' can quietly give rise to ego—the belief that we are the central force behind everything. For example, someone might think, 'I earn money for my family,' a wife might feel, 'I manage everything in the kitchen,' or children might say, 'We serve the family.' These thoughts reflect a sense of ego, where we believe, we are the primary force behind these actions and their results.

To understand this better, consider the story of a wise spiritual teacher and a powerful king. The king had recently conquered many regions and was praised throughout his kingdom. Proud of his accomplishments, he visited his teacher and spoke of how his efforts had brought peace and prosperity to his people.

The guru, seeing the pride in the king's words, took him for a walk in the nearby forest. There, he pointed to a large rock and asked the king to break the rock open. Inside the rock, they found a living frog. The guru then asked, 'Who kept this frog alive inside a sealed rock? Was it your effort or planning?' The guru explained that the frog survived by its own karma and fortune, not because of anyone's intervention. He gently reminded the king, not to fall into the illusion of control or superiority. Just as the frog lives by its own destiny, so too does every being. We are participants in a larger system, not the sole cause of outcomes. The message was clear: true greatness is grounded in humility.

This story teaches us humility and the recognition that, while we may contribute to outcomes, we are not the sole creators. Understanding this helps us overcome ego, and see our actions as part of a larger context. For example, if a lizard were to believe it is holding up the ceiling, it would be living under the illusion of self-importance. Recognising our true role helps diminish the ego.

When a person acts out of duty, they will not have expectations. Expectations arise when someone thinks, 'I am doing all this for others.' There are two possible scenarios: doing nothing for others and everything for yourself, or repaying a past favour. In both cases, you are ultimately doing it for your own benefit. For example, repaying a bank loan is not a favour to the bank; it benefits you. Similarly, raising children is not a favour; it secures your emotional or practical future. If you think, 'I did my duty, and my child did not reciprocate,' it will only lead to disappointment.

Expectations lead to dissatisfaction. The solution to handling unfulfilled expectations is to look inward and focus on the soul. We have to understand that the results we experience are the outcomes of our past actions. We should view our responsibilities as duties, not as favours and remember, that we are reaping what we ourselves sowed in the past. By shifting our perspective from ego and expectation to soul and duty, we can reduce our emotional dependency and avoid the sorrows that stems from unmet expectations.

Actionables

- Who controls your laughter, smiles, tears, sadness, stress, worries, and happiness? List down their name(s).
- If you cannot completely control your expectations, can you reduce them? Write down how.

Reminders:

- Whenever expectations arise, they bring nothing but sorrow.
- Others do not cause you sadness; your expectations do.
- To live without expectations means, keeping your remote control in your own hands, not in someone else's.
- Expectations arise when someone thinks that they are the central force behind everything—'I am doing all this.'
- By shifting our focus inward and prioritising our soul, we can reduce expectations and achieve contentment.

MANAGE YOUR EXPECTATIONS

IN THE PREVIOUS CHAPTER, WE LEARNED HOW TO perform our duties without becoming overly attached to them. This detachment helps protect us from the burden of expectations. As our sense of doership increases, so do our expectations. But is it possible to live without any expectations? It is difficult but not impossible. By maintaining constant awareness and diligence in our duties, we can gradually rise above expectations and move closer to a more peaceful, God-centred life.

In practical life, however, living and interacting with others inevitably gives rise to expectations. While we can try to prevent them, expectations often creep in. Since eliminating them entirely is not always realistic, the next best approach is to manage them. Manage your expectations. Organise and determine—how many and from whom, we should have expectations. Finding this balance is crucial. When we expect from others, we must also have expectations from ourselves. Healthy self-expectations can serve as motivation, pushing us toward growth and achievement.

Everyone has expectations but often lacks the capabilities to meet them—whether for themselves or others. First deserve, then desire. Focus on building your capabilities, before creating expectations. Before forming expectations, focus on building your own capabilities. As your strengths grow, the need for constant desires naturally diminishes. Those who are capable often do not need to ask for much. For instance, if you consistently give your best effort at work, recognition and reward—like a salary increase—tend to follow. But if you do not have the capability, then why have expectations? This concept applies everywhere—in the workplace, in social settings, in a temple, and even among friends. As expectations arise, make sure your capabilities are rising alongside them.

Let us talk about relationships. When do you start to feel hurt or experience conflict with someone close to you? Often, it stems from over-expectation. When we expect too much, complications arise. For example, if you come home from work expecting a good meal and do not get it, you may feel upset. Even if your expectation is genuine, it's important to ask: 'Does the person I'm expecting from actually have the capacity to meet this need?' Sometimes, our expectations exceed the other person's abilities. This mismatch can lead to disappointment and conflict. Expectations become especially harmful when we expect more from someone than they can realistically give, creating emotional tension and potentially damaging the relationship.

In Jain philosophy, the concept of अनेकांतवाद (*anekantavada)*—the idea of multiple viewpoints—encourages greater understanding and balance in our interactions. People often see the world only through their own perspective, which leads to misunderstandings and conflicts. To resolve this, try viewing situations from the other person's angle, considering their circumstances emotions, and limitations. Imagine viewing a building from different angles—front, left, right, and rear. Each perspective is unique. If you and your spouse see the building from opposite sides, your descriptions will differ. To truly understand each other, you need to switch places and see what the other sees. This is the essence of anekantavada, and embracing it can transform your perspective and improve your relationships.

In real life, conflicts often arise when both parties stick to their own viewpoints. Instead, try to see the situation from the other person's perspective. For instance, if someone comes home after a long, stressful day and seems irritable, you might think, 'Why is he always yelling?' Meanwhile, he's thinking, 'I've had such a tough day.' Both perspectives are valid, but without understanding each other's experiences, conflict is likely to follow. Recognising and respecting multiple viewpoints is the key to harmony.

Understanding this can resolve many problems. The goal is not to eliminate expectations entirely, but to set them at the right level: zero, moderate, or high, based on the person's capabilities. If someone is capable, high expectations may be appropriate. But if they are not, even moderate expectations can lead to disappointment. In such situations, it is best to keep your expectations at zero. So, ask yourself: 'Which category do I fall into—zero, moderate, or high?'

A person's nature is intrinsic, like a colour that cannot be changed. Green will always be green, and red will always be red. So why expect green to turn red? The issue arises when we try to change someone's fundamental nature. If someone is naturally like the red colour, accept them as red. Rather than trying to transform them, focus on understanding whether they are a red, green, or yellow type of person. Acceptance, not resistance, leads to peace.

Beyond capability, we must also consider external factors such as environment and life circumstances. For instance, a talented student from a poor background might work six to eight hours a day to support his family, making it difficult for him to attend college regularly. While his ability is high, expecting top academic performance may be unrealistic given his situation. This shows how context must shape our expectations.

Capability can be improved. Everyone has the potential to excel, but some may have forgotten it. A positive, motivating environment can help awaken their inner hidden potential. Sometimes, capabilities are dormant or unconscious, and need the right conditions to be awakened. Seeing others progress can sometimes inspire them, to realise and use their capabilities.

Living with low expectations brings in a lot of happiness. If you expect your child to score 80 per cent but know that the child was sick and could not study much, yet, they score 82 per cent, you will be happy. However, consider the thought processes at play: when you expect 95 per cent and the child scores 88 per cent, you might be disappointed but the child might be happy with 88 per cent, because they see it as a good result—given the effort they could put in under the circumstances.

In life, be it relationships between the husband-wife, parent-child, or work, or the society, we often carry high expectations, without fully understanding the other person's situation or capabilities. So, we need to learn how to manage our expectations—learning how much to expect from others and from ourselves. People often complain about the behaviour of others, but we should become aware of this tendency and consciously adjust our expectations—to be more realistic and considerate of others circumstances and abilities. This understanding can lead to healthier relationships, and a more balanced, contented life.

When we constantly demand or complain, we gain little. Instead, by focusing on developing our own potential, we reduce our reliance on others—and often, people naturally come forward to support us. Believe in your abilities and trust that they will bring you what you truly deserve. This approach may take time, but it works. Letting go of rigid expectations brings people closer, while demanding or forcing things makes others uncomfortable. You may have often felt disappointed by expecting too much from others. Try working without expectations. You will benefit more if your intentions are pure. Perform your duties selflessly, and if expectations arise, ensure they align with the other person's abilities and situation.

When you start caring for others' feelings and situations, they will do everything for you, without being asked to. If you want someone to feel close to you, win their heart with love, not demands. No one truly become yours through demands. If someone acts out of fear or obligation, they may complete the task, but it won't come from a place of devotion. Their actions will be mechanical, driven by a desire to avoid conflict rather than genuine commitment.

Another important aspect is clarity. If you expect something from someone, they should be aware of your feelings and expectations. There should be clarity. Sometimes, we assume others understand our feelings or needs, but if we have not clearly expressed them, misunderstandings are bound to happen. This confusion can cause unnecessary tension. Ideally, being completely free of expectations is the best. However, if you do have expectations, make sure you communicate them. After all, if the other person does not know what you expect or how you feel, how can they respond appropriately? Clear, honest communication can prevent many problems and bring people closer together.

Another important point to consider is whether your expectations are realistic. Sometimes, you may expect something completely unreasonable. For example, in your family, if you compare your child's handwriting with another child's, you might overlook your child's unique strengths, such as better grasping power. Every person has their own talents and strengths. No one is an all-rounder in everything. For instance, in a cricket match, you would not expect a bowler to excel at batting or a batsman to be a great bowler. If you see someone who is an all-rounder, it does not mean everyone can be one. If you start expecting your child to be good at everything, like batting, bowling, and fielding, it is unrealistic. Each person has unique abilities, and it is important to recognise and appreciate those individual strengths instead of making unfair comparisons.

Not everyone excels in every area. Each person has their own specialties and expertise in their respective fields. So why do you compare their expertise to that of your child's or other family member's? Try to understand their expertise neutrally. In the field where they have expertise, you can expect a ten out of ten, but why do you expect a ten out of ten in areas where they have no background or natural skill? No matter how much effort they put in, they will not be able to deliver the result you are hoping for. When you set high expectations for being an all-rounder, it can lead to disappointment.

For example, you might expect your child to excel in math, science, social science, and even be good in temple activities, performing rituals, and taking care of you. But why expect one child to embody the strengths of many different children, each excelling in different areas? Expecting 100 per cent in every field without considering where their expertise lies, is unreasonable. It is better to set high expectations in areas where they are naturally skilled, and adjust your expectations in others. Perhaps they are less organised in keeping their clothes or school bag tidy—but that does not mean they lack ability elsewhere.

Take your husband as an example. He may not accompany you to the temple, but if he respects your choice and never stops you from going, that in itself is something to appreciate. While he may not actively participate in rituals, he might still live with integrity, kindness, and respect for others. Learn to appreciate people for their strengths in their fields. When we start appreciating others in their areas of expertise, they become more aligned with us, and once they are, you can ask them to do whatever you wish.

If you find it hard to rise above your expectations, learn how to manage them properly. Expectation is not the problem; the problem is the benchmark we set in our minds for others. We want others to meet the fixed standard we have set. Every person desires others to be all-rounder. However, consider how you yourself are perceived. Do you deliver what you expect from others? First, become an all-rounder yourself before expecting it from others. It is important to realise that not everyone will become an all-rounder, because they might not have the capabilities or the resources required. So, do not expect something beyond their nature as people will often remain true to it. If something is red, it will always be red; if something is green, it will always be green.

Ultimately, the most important thing is to align your expectations with what is realistic. First, adjust yourself according to what you expect from others, and then expect it from them. We often want others to change completely, while we remain rigid ourselves. If you want to fulfil your expectations, the best approach is to first make the other person feel valued—with humility, respect, love, service, and appreciation. When we bend a little, the other person is also more likely to bend a bit. This way, your expectations will be managed properly; otherwise, you will remain unhappy.

Actionables

- **Identify expectations:**

Who do you have the highest expectations from in your life? List these individuals, starting with those whom you spend the most time with. Reflect on the areas where you feel unhappy or troubled.

- **Reflect on expectations from your spouse:**

In which areas, do you have expectations from your spouse? What are the common reasons for your arguments? Have you ever taken time to think about this?

- **Evaluate appropriateness of expectations:**

Are your expectations aligned with the capabilities others have, or are they unrealistic?

- **Consider their perspective:**

Have you ever tried to understand things from your coworker's or family member's point of view?

Reminders:

- If you cannot rise above your expectations, learn how to manage them properly.
- Adopt the perspective of anekantavada—multiplicity of viewpoints, which promotes understanding and balance.
- First deserve, then desire. Focus on building your capabilities before creating expectations. When you develop your abilities, the need for desires diminishes.
- Perform your duties selflessly, and if you need to have expectations, align them with the other person's abilities and situation.

ACCEPTANCE: THE KEY TO TRUE HAPPINESS

Everyone yearns for a life filled with joy and devoid of stress, regardless of their external circumstances. However, it appears that even those who possess wealth, or success often experience discontentment and unhappiness. The main reason for this unhappiness is because people often struggle to accept things as they are. It is important to have an attitude of acceptance towards what is happening in one's life. Resisting or rejecting circumstances can breed anxiety, while embracing them opens the door to discovering solutions. Having a mindset of acceptance helps you deal with challenges positively. But the failure to accept circumstances can complicate problem-solving and finding solutions. Mastering the art of embracing situations as they unfold, is a fundamental aspect of attaining long-lasting happiness.

Today, everyone faces challenges in relationships, health, work, and finances. Unhappiness often stems from non-acceptance, while combining acceptance with these challenges brings positive emotions. Embracing life's difficulties—whether fear, anger, jealousy, or illness—is crucial. Acceptance transforms weaknesses into strengths, turning adversity into opportunities for growth and resilience.

Realising our challenges is the first step to finding solutions. Our focus has to be on what we can control. In situations beyond our control, like the family we are born into, embracing acceptance becomes crucial. Many people tend to live in a state of non-acceptance, especially when faced with worries. Worrying indicates a refusal to accept the situation, similar to chasing a dog away. Even when it is a small dog that may not be running well, yet people still react by running upon seeing it. Likewise, in life such a behaviour signifies a lack of acceptance, and a tendency to resist the present circumstances.

विपाक-विचय धर्म ध्यान *(vipak-vichay dharma dhyana)*, as per Jain scriptures, advocates for accepting life's problems and providing solutions for various challenges—whether physical, mental, or arising from factors like, the environment, relationships, or parenting. Introspection is crucial for prompting individuals to identify the root cause of their sadness during difficulties. This process of self-analysis prompts reflection on reactions to various situations, developing a deeper understanding, and equipping individuals to address challenges with resilience and wisdom.

Acceptance is pivotal in navigating life's unexpected challenges. When confronting health issues at a young age, initial feelings of anxiety and concern can be transformed into long-term solutions through acceptance. Accepting a disease is the first step to finding solutions, and prompting suggestions such as, consulting a doctor or changing eating or sleeping habits. Learning to accept challenges, opens doors to understanding, coping, and seeking solutions. Facing a disease, even a severe one like cancer, requires essential acceptance, recognising that certain aspects are beyond our control, and embracing the reality for a more peaceful mindset.

Further, the decision to accept or reject plays a pivotal role, in shaping our emotional responses to the accomplishments of others. Seeing someone else's progress and feeling jealous often originates from an inability to tolerate their success. However, acknowledging and accepting a colleague or batchmate's achievements, can transform them into sources of inspiration and motivation. Conversely, refusing to accept their success can fuel jealousy, causing the negative emotion to intensify within oneself. This negative mindset starts small but grows over time, hindering one's creativity and problem-solving capabilities. Thus, embracing acceptance allows us to clear roadblocks, and become the architects of success. It is within our power to view others as stepping stones rather than stumbling blocks—contingent on our ability to accept and appreciate others' qualities.

In relationships, if your partner or child displays certain behaviours, why not accept them? Dwelling on unfairness and blaming others is unproductive; instead, focus on what is within your control. If you have been evading these situations for five to ten years, living in a constant state of tension, unable to sleep through the night, experiencing rising blood pressure and elevated sugar levels, and feeling a sense of loss, consider that many individuals find themselves in similar predicaments. True happiness in life, often arises when we learn to accept the circumstances we face. Learn to adapt to unchanging circumstances, and channel that energy towards proactive actions rather than dwelling on the past.

Further, acceptance also leads to forgiveness when anger arises from unmet expectations. By acknowledging one's own capabilities and understanding the uniqueness of every individual, one adopts acceptance, and dispels unrealistic expectations. Embracing your body's nature and refraining from comparisons, allows for effective problem-solving in life.

While striving for the best is essential, acceptance becomes crucial when efforts do not yield results. It is not about avoiding hard work or turning away from duty, but recognising that, despite one's best efforts, outcomes may not always align with expectations. Immediate acceptance may not be necessary initially, but eventually acknowledging setbacks and learning from them is vital. Individuals commonly experience failures and drawbacks even after putting in hard work, and acceptance in these situations becomes the key to personal growth and resilience.

Acceptance is pivotal for overcoming distress and avoiding an inferiority complex. Solutions only become apparent once you start embracing acceptance, while running away, denying, and blaming only perpetuates your problems. Acknowledging and accepting the situation rather than grumbling, leads to constructive solutions. The key to finding solutions lies in acceptance, whether it is managing a short temper or facing challenges. Transforming negative emotions requires acknowledging and accepting our circumstances, and turning weaknesses into strengths.

Positivity aligns with acceptance, while negativity arises from non-acceptance. Happiness stems from learning to accept and letting go of anger, despair, and jealousy. Living in acceptance mode is the key to inner peace and well-being.

Actionables

- Identify five emotions causing stress in your life, and consider how embracing acceptance, can turn them into sources of happiness.
- Write down five positive qualities of a person you envy, and explore how these attributes, can serve as inspiration and motivation for your own personal growth.
- Identify five situations that are beyond your control that add negativity, and explore the possibility of easing their impact through the practice of acceptance.

Reminders:

- Something or someone plus acceptance, leads to experiencing positive emotions.
- Something or someone plus rejection, leads to experiencing negative emotions.
- Acceptance is crucial in overcoming distress. Solutions emerge when you are embracing acceptance, while running away, denying, and blaming only perpetuates these problems.

WAY TO ACHIEVING ACCEPTANCE

IN THE PRECEDING CHAPTER, WE EXPLORED THE CONCEPT that nurturing happiness and maintaining a stress-free lifestyle in all circumstances, involves embracing an attitude of acceptance. To live a content and tension-free life, it is crucial to learn the art of accepting—with full awareness—what comes our way, whether favourable or unfavourable. As we begin to perceive situations for what they truly are, and wholeheartedly embrace acceptance, we open ourselves to a deeper, more lasting sense of joy.

Here, an argument arises. Understanding acceptance seems relatively simple; however, when real-life situations unfold, we often overlook these principles. In the heat of the moment, we get swept away, and the challenges of the circumstances weigh heavily on us. Now the question arises: can we implement an attitude of acceptance effectively, even during such critical moments?

Achieving success requires more than just planning—it demands execution. While planning is undoubtedly an initial step in the success of any endeavour, it alone does not accomplish much. In the lives of 99 per cent of individuals, plans often stay as they are—without any actual implementation. Once the execution phase commences, our thoughts, desires, and aspirations take on practical form. This transformation is the catalyst for success and the generator of joy. The crucial question now arises: which path should we choose, and what steps should we take, to ensure the successful implementation of an attitude of acceptance from within?

At times, accepting certain situations becomes a challenge as our minds resist embracing them. Let us explore—how we can grasp the concept of acceptance, integrate it into our lives, and develop the ability to put it into practice.

In everyday life, we commonly observe that individuals struggle with acceptance in about four or five situations even when they intellectually understand the need for it. The first scenario arises, when an event triggers immediate anger and the individual struggles to control it. The second scenario involves jealousy emerging within us, instead of being motivated by the progress of others. The third scenario entails facing separation from someone in our life—which proves to be challenging—and our heart finds it difficult to accept such events. In the fourth scenario, the discovery of a major disease leaves us unprepared to cope with it. The fifth scenario pertains to those business situations where a substantial financial loss occurs, and recovery seems impossible. Some individuals even experience heart failure due to such circumstances. These are just a few examples. Life often presents situations where, despite our awareness and understanding, acceptance feels out of reach.

Now, let us take this a step further through a meaningful practical exercise, where you reflect on the significant questions below—which are the inevitable ultimate truths of your life. Work on effectively integrating an attitude of acceptance during these critical moments. The more honestly and openly you engage, the more prepared you will become to face life's uncertainties with peace and resilience.

Reflective Questions:

- What are the things that you cannot accept in your life?
- If your spouse were to pass away, what impact would it have on you, and how long do you think the grief would persist?
- If your wife were to be diagnosed with a serious illness and the situation became dire, how long do you think the pain would last for you?
- How long do you believe the grief would endure within you, if you were to face the loss of your son to cancer while you are still alive?
- Anything we are most attached to, the one we cherish the most, and without which life appears challenging—what will occur if it is lost?
- Suppose, you get liver cancer detected at an advanced stage; what are your preparations to face it?
- Anger often arises instantly when we encounter something we find unacceptable or unpleasant. If you

struggle to manage such emotions, how can you train your mind to remain composed during those moments?

The key solution to overcome the primary challenges is learning acceptance, and developing the ability to visualise—what may unfold in our future. Learning to anticipate and mentally prepare for the worst is essential, considering potential challenges in our lives. It is important to comprehend the worst-case scenarios and develop strategies to navigate through them. The fundamental principle remains: those who are prepared can effectively handle shocks, while those unprepared feel the impact more profoundly.

The most effective approach is, to cultivate the habit of advance preparation. This includes two areas: one, preparing for what might happen in the future, and two, preparing for what is certain to happen. People often neglect to prepare for what might happen, because it carries a probability—it may or may not occur. However, it is essential to focus on preparing for the inevitable ultimate truth. Prioritising preparation for these inevitable events can build emotional resilience and stability.

A crucial part of this preparation involves setting realistic expectations. People behave according to their nature—so it makes sense to accept them as they are. Instead of resisting their natural tendencies, ask yourself: 'Why don't I simply accept that this person's nature is different from mine?' We often fall into the trap of expecting a tortoise to swim like a fish, a monkey to sit still like a tortoise, a crow to sing like a cuckoo, or a lion to eat leaves like an elephant. But whose mistake is that—ours or theirs? If you sit beneath a mango tree expecting oranges to fall, you will be disappointed forever. Acceptance begins with setting the right expectations.

Understanding the value of acceptance leads to peace. The journey begins with self-awareness—evaluating ourselves first—and from there, inspiring growth in others. Acceptance nurtures inner strength and emotional clarity. When practiced consistently over time—even just six months—it can lead to profound inner transformation and a more peaceful life.

Actionables

Analyse each scenario from the table below:

First scenario	Second scenario	Third scenario	Fourth scenario
If my spouse passes away, what impact would it have on me or vice-versa, and how long would the grief persist?	If I get a major disease, what will be the effect on me and my family members?	In which situations am I getting the angriest; how am I reacting and how can I overcome it?	Are my expectations from anyone justified?

Analyse the impact on spouse/ Son/ Daughter/ Parents/ Siblings/ Other Relatives/ Friend/ Boss/ Team-mates/ Society	Am I prepared to face it?	List down what things make you angry and on whom you get angry.	Analyse: Do I expect a cuckoo from a crow, a tortoise from a monkey, or an orange from a mango?

Reminders:

- The key solution to overcome the primary challenge is to learn acceptance, and develop the ability to visualise what will unfold in our future.
- People often neglect to prepare for what might happen because it carries a probability—it may or may not occur. However, it is essential to focus on preparing for the inevitable ultimate truth.
- Embracing acceptance fosters inner strength.

SOLUTIONS FOR ACCEPTANCE

THE PRECEDING CHAPTER HIGHLIGHTED THE importance of embracing acceptance, which cultivates inner strength, prepares us for the unavoidable ultimate truth and enhances our ability to foresee what lies ahead in our future. Our minds are not readily inclined to accept reality; we often resist acknowledging reality. Instead, we often perceive things based on preconceived notions. Deep-rooted thoughts within us form a sort of inner reality, and individuals shape their lives in a manner that makes anything contrary seem intolerable.

We often dwell in an imaginary world, where we have anchored our sense of reality. However, true joy cannot thrive in this imaginary realm. Regardless of how delightful the dream may seem; true joy remains elusive. Once we wake up, the illusion dissolves and disappears. During sleep, one might believe, 'My life is wonderful; everything in my family is perfect.' While this may be true in the dream, it is short-lived. Dreams are fleeting, and if we mistake them for reality, this misunderstanding persists within us.

There are two types of dreams: one that unfolds with closed eyes, relatively harmless upon awakening; and another that transpires with open eyes, potentially dangerous. The latter is a creation of the imaginative realm within our minds. Individuals rooted in their comfort zones resist stepping out, unprepared to confront changes in their surroundings. Until there is internal acceptance and adaptation, persistent dissatisfaction prevails.

Let us embrace the reality now. The past is like a dream, the present is ours to live, and the future is just something we imagine. If we dwell in the past or constantly look to the future, we are avoiding the present, and that leads to trouble and unhappiness. When we escape the present, we lose our balance. It is important to develop the habit of living in the moment. Our experiences and awareness are rooted in the present—the things we go through right now, the past is our memory, and the future is our imagination. We can remember past events, but the experience is always happening in the present. For instance, if you enjoyed some delicious sweets yesterday, you can remember the moment, but you cannot taste it now. The taste only comes, when you are eating it in the present. True joy is created when you are fully present in that moment.

Often, we believe that understanding a situation is enough—but when life truly tests us, it becomes clear that understanding is not the same as acceptance. Reality can be harsh, unexpected, and unkind. Accepting it—especially when it deviates from our ideals—is not easy. Why is that?

The challenge lies in the fact that most of us live more in our expectations than in the real world. We build ideal scenarios in our minds: a peaceful family life, well-behaved children, stable health, and consistent financial success. These visions give us comfort, but they also create fragility. A minor illness in a child becomes overwhelming. A small quarrel in the household disrupts our peace. A dip in the market feels catastrophic when we are emotionally invested in constant gains.

The truth is, we are not mentally prepared. Not for illness, not for loss, not even for inconvenience. It is not that these events are rare—but that we have not trained ourselves to expect them. And when reality deviates from our imagination, the emotional cost is far higher.

Mental preparedness does not mean becoming pessimistic or emotionally distant. It means cultivating the internal strength to accept that life comes with setbacks and surprises. It means building resilience—not just knowledge. It is the capacity to stand steady when things do not go your way.

Successful people, particularly in business, understand this. They do not assume every venture will succeed. Their preparedness softens the shock of failure. Likewise, emotional resilience in life comes from recognising that relationships will test us, that health can falter, and that even the best-laid plans may derail.

Mental training starts by aligning our expectations with life's uncertainties. We must learn to see things as they are, not as we wish them to be. This alignment allows us to respond with composure, rather than being swept away by distress.

To learn to accept the world and confront challenges, we need to delve within ourselves. Look at history, look at the great personalities whom you consider as your role models. Their lives are shaped by navigating numerous ups and downs. A true role model is not someone who sails smoothly through life, but one who faces adversity and struggles. Inspiration comes from those who have endured irregularities and adversities, demonstrating resilience and perseverance. A feeling must arise within, that when our role model can accomplish this, we too can achieve it.

Life is about overcoming adversities. The greater one's awareness, alertness, and vigilance, the smoother one handles circumstances. Conversely, negligence and living in delusion lead to heightened shocks. A vigilant person confronts situations with open eyes, embracing them with equanimity rooted in experience, not imagination. Understanding that the body changes is essential, as the world operates on the law of change; nothing remains static. Yesterday is not today, and today will not be tomorrow.

Embracing this reality is crucial. Why do we often evade the truth? Like a cat closing its eyes while drinking milk, presuming invisibility, people often escape from reality, thinking that if they cannot see it, it does not exist. This avoidance, like the cat's behaviour, raises the question: Why should one live in denial? Why not confront reality with open eyes?

Contemplating things beyond our control is futile; it accomplishes nothing. For instance, unfavourable weather, heavy rain, and the rising spread of diseases, and viruses—are uncontrollable factors. Differentiate between what is within your control and what is not. Create two columns: list things beyond your control in the first column and things that are controllable but often neglected in the second column. You will realise that 60-70 per cent of your concerns fall in the first column. Acknowledge this, as constant disturbance arises from futile worries. Take responsibility for what is within your control. For instance, to combat mosquito-borne illnesses, get engaged in cleanliness campaigns. Regarding infectious diseases like Covid-19, focus on proactive measures within your reach. Acknowledge what you can do and act upon it. Problems may or may not exist, but you have created some of them. If we learn to see this and learn to leave it, we will find a new path from there.

When challenges start appearing in our lives and we are unable to accept them, one should prepare themselves and engage in activities that bring you joy. Here are some solutions:

- Cultivate your feelings, accepting them as they are. Repeat the lines, 'Whatever happens, happens; it is what it is. How does it matter to us?' with a calm mind, practicing in the morning and before sleeping. This repetition is a valuable exercise for your subconscious mind, and gradually shapes your nature. Recognise that awareness and mindfulness develop gradually through consistent practice, transforming you over time.
- Meditation cultivates alert observation, making the mental state resilient. This resilience diminishes the power of circumstances to bring you down, enabling individuals to view situations objectively.

- Stop the habit of comparing. When you find yourself envious of others, transform it into joy by recognising their virtues and happiness. Observe others not to feel inferior, but to identify qualities within them, that can manifest in you. This mindset keeps you in a receptive mode.
- Embrace healthy competition and avoid harbouring feelings of inferiority. Set goals based on your capabilities.
- In real life, view successful individuals as role models.
- Creativity flourishes in a relaxed, stress-free state, while stress hampers the ability to create meaningfully.
- Cultivate a sense of compassion, peace, forgiveness, and generosity within yourself.
- In the realm of medical science, emphasise self-cure, which empowers us to combat challenges.
- Cultivate patience to enhance tolerance.
- Deliberate on the after-effects of emotions like anger, jealousy, greed, misbehaviour, and anxiety.
- Embrace the principle of anekantavada (the doctrine of non-absolutism), and contemplate how you would respond in that situation considering other's perspectives.
- Despite diligent efforts, success may seem elusive. When the body does not cooperate, financial losses occur, or betrayal is faced, contemplate the principle of कर्म सिद्धांत *(karma siddhant)* or the doctrine of karma. The outcome of our actions is certain to manifest.

The chapter guides individuals toward acceptance by emphasising the importance of living in the present, cultivating mindfulness through meditation, and adopting principles that promote resilience and inner strength in the face of life's challenges. We often dwell in imagination, anticipating whether our wishes will come true someday. The question arises: Why do we persist in this imaginative space? Why do we not connect with reality?

While we invest substantial effort in the pursuit of excellence in various aspects of life, it is crucial to acknowledge that if success remains elusive, it might be worthwhile to contemplate letting go. Recognising that certain elements are beyond our control is integral to our fate. Within the constraints of those circumstances, our best course of action is to strive for excellence, and make the most of the opportunities presented.

Actionables

- Distinguish between what is in your control and what is not.

Things beyond your control	Controllable things but often neglected

- How do you rate yourself in preparedness to take any future shock, and unhappiness on a scale of one to ten (one being least and ten being most)?
- What problems do you have in life that are self-created by your thinking?

Reminders:

- We need to live in the present, as dwelling in the past or future leads to discontent.
- Meditation is a powerful tool to become an alert observer, unaffected by external circumstances, and helps in developing awareness, vigilance, and equanimity.
- Certain elements that are beyond our control, are integral to our fate.

EMBRACING ACCEPTANCE THROUGH MEDITATION

In the preceding chapters, our focus has been on comprehending acceptance—the key to a content and joyful life. We explored how to cultivate a sense of acceptance, examining the solutions that can be generated internally by navigating diverse situations. Implementing acceptance enriches our lives with profound joy, urging us to integrate this sentiment into our daily existence. Regardless of the form or condition in which life presents itself, embracing it without complaint or grumbling leads to a tension-free existence. Although challenging, adopting this mindset is crucial.

Life often unfolds in unfavourable circumstances, with individuals holding varying ideologies. Conflicts arise when our thoughts diverge from those around us, whether in the family, workplace, or society. Aligning differing perspectives is no easy feat, and maintaining happiness amidst such discord is daunting.

The most effective solution lies in cultivating complete awareness and internal alertness. By adopting the role of a witness detached from events, and accepting them as they are, we can minimise worry. Observing situations from a distance, much like viewing an object from afar, shields us from undue influence. Closer proximity amplifies the impact, leading to both positive and negative consequences.

Deep attachment gives rise to feelings of hatred and tension. Excessive attachment eventually transforms into resentment. It is akin to only sweet things that attract ants; so, eliminating sweetness eradicates the problem. Similarly, reducing attachment mitigates the emergence of negative emotions.

Remaining unaffected requires developing a mindset, that allows events to unfold naturally. Becoming an observer and knower—devoid of complaints, and adopting an attitude of contentment and acceptance, facilitates resilience. Consistent affirmation and practice enhance this mindset. While complete immunity to external influences may be challenging, adopting a slightly detached perspective offers some relief.

Tolerance becomes a powerful tool in remaining happy despite adverse circumstances. Initiating the practice of tolerance, affirming one's chosen mindset, and cultivating resilience allow individuals to weather difficulties with grace. This shift takes time, but the gradual transition becomes apparent.

Every person's emotional response is shaped by the intersection of matter, space, and time. Interactions with others evoke laughter, tears, or anger based on the observer's emotional state. When we find ourselves unable to control our reactions—based on others actions, words, or behaviour—it signifies that we have relinquished control of our autonomy and emotional well-being to external forces. Exercising a bit of detachment is akin to keeping our metaphorical remote control in our own hands. No one should have the power to manipulate our emotions or dictate our responses; we ought to remain true to ourselves and not succumb to external pressures and influences.

True happiness stems from within, and our goal should be to cultivate such positive emotions in our inner world. Consistent practice of acceptance yields remarkable results, making it easier to overcome adversity. A genuine person who embraces this practice daily will witness remarkable changes in their life. While the process requires time, the transformative effects gradually become evident in one's life.

Actionables

- Engage in the practice of cultivating feelings of acceptance through meditation.
- Begin by visualising situations where you feel a lack of control or experience negativity. Instead of generalising, focus on specific individuals—family members, colleagues, or society members—with whom

disagreements arise. As you visualise, actively cultivate a sense of acceptance towards everyone involved, fostering a mindset that problems will not overpower you.

- Reiterate these affirmations regularly to foster positive change from within:
    - 'I harbour no grievances towards anyone or anything.'
    - 'I wholeheartedly accept what I have received.'
    - 'I embrace my circumstances as they are.'
    - 'I am completely content with my present situation.'
    - 'I am free from worries.'
    - 'I release all expectations from others.'

Reminders:

- Meditation on acceptance becomes a powerful tool in this journey. By visualising and accepting specific situations, we can gradually overcome challenges. This practice instils a sense of calmness, providing solutions to problems rather than allowing them to fester in the realm of non-acceptance.
- Consistent repetition of the recommended affirmations leads to an internal transformation, gradually aligning our thoughts and actions, attracting positive energies, and influencing our outlook on life.

PART 3

OVERCOMING BARRIERS

ESCAPE THE OVERTHINKING TRAP

THE IMPACT OF OUR THOUGHTS ON OUR LIVES IS significant. The thoughts that arise in our minds determine the direction, shaping the trajectory and defining the outcome of our lives. No individual is entirely devoid of thoughts; even in moments of quietude or when we close our eyes. Our mind is always active, like a machine that never takes a break. We can't completely get away from our thoughts. You might be familiar with various forms of thinking—positive thinking, negative thinking, overthinking, and unnecessary thinking. So, our thought processes can fluctuate between positivity and undesired areas, which we might wish to avoid. Now, how do we differentiate whether our thinking is organised or not?

The term overthinking is described as, 'repeatedly dwelling on the same matter, often leading to negative thoughts.' Some thoughts and ideas fall within our control, while others lie beyond, challenging our ability to control them. Another form of thinking is unnecessary thinking, where a person ponders illogically over irrelevant matters, yielding no sensible conclusions. It involves contemplating unrealistic scenarios, like, 'If I were the prime minister, I would do this or that.' Negative thinking represents a sudden onset of low spirits and disappointment, even when one seemingly has everything in life. When negative thinking intensifies, it can lead to thoughts of self-harm or suicide—causing both physical and mental health issues, often leading to depression. On the brighter side, when thoughts are positive, they constructively influence a person's life. Naturally, nobody desires to lead a disorganised life. Most people aspire to have a life filled with positivity in their thoughts. Do you share a similar aspiration for your life?

At times, despite our efforts to stay positive, our minds seem resistant. Many set resolutions like 'I'll think positively,' yet their minds start drifting elsewhere within a few minutes. Even in moments of meditating or chanting mantras, the mind continues to wander. Have you ever wondered why our minds are not easily controlled? We should ideally guide our minds, yet often, it feels like the mind is guiding us. We aspire to lead our thoughts, believing that directing the mind will steer it where we want. Are we influenced by thoughts, or do we influence them? Where does our thoughts and emotions originate from?

In psychological terms, when something deeply ingrains into the subconscious mind, it shapes our habits. These strong impressions lead a person to repeat actions, often losing control over them. This repetitive behaviour embeds the same patterns of thinking, contributing to persistent overthinking. Even when external circumstances seem fine, internal emotions can trigger anxiety. It is a cycle of continuous and repetitive contemplation about various matters.

Let us get some insights from the story of a highly educated individual, who was working in a prestigious IT company earning a lucrative salary, yet constantly burdened by stress and frustration due to overthinking and an overwhelming workload. Seeking guidance, he turned to a saint who assigned a task to him of an unusual solution. The saint advised him to manage a group of camels for a night, instructing him to sleep only when all the camels slept. As the man attempted to synchronise the camels' rest, he found it challenging and could not sleep. This experience made him realise that like managing the camels' sleep, life's problems cannot always be instantly resolved. It requires time and patience.

The story emphasises the importance of living in the present, addressing challenges one step at a time, and understanding that not all problems can be solved immediately. Some issues, like the camels, may be managed, while others—despite earnest efforts—might remain unsolvable.

In another story, a father gave his child a seed, and instructed him to plant it in a pot. He explained, 'This seed will grow into a beautiful plant.' Excitedly, the child planted the seed and eagerly checked the soil daily, hoping to see signs of growth. Continuously digging to check for progress, the child became disappointed when nothing emerged. Over time the seed dried up. The key to its successful growth was to plant the seed once, water it consistently, and then let nature take its course. Growth happens at its own pace, and sometimes it requires patience without constant interference.

Overthinking about the potential results of our actions at every moment does not change anything. Why not consider adopting a wait-and-watch policy? Life presents a myriad of challenges, and time often acts as a powerful healer. Allowing situations to unfold with patience, frequently leads to their resolution. However, quick thinking and impulsive actions may not yield the intended outcomes. Supplying an entire two-month water quota to a single tree will not magically produce fruit. Similarly, facing an illness and taking a week's dosage in a single day can result in more harm than good.

Consider, why your energy is repeatedly invested in thought processes that yield no results. While you exert efforts, not all problems may be under your influence. Some issues naturally resolve themselves over time. When we discuss the concept of thinking, it should align with effective planning, a defined goal, and a structured roadmap. Our approach should involve determining how to create maps, deciding on the appropriate steps, when to make decisions, and what decisions to make. However, well-educated individuals with abundant resources, amenities, and a substantial income often overthink the most, and fail to implement their plans. On the other hand, individuals earning daily wages and grappling with hand-to-mouth survival often live in the present, focusing on basic sustenance and finding contentment in simple pleasures.

Irrespective of whether it pertains to your goals, projects, job, or business, the trap of overthinking persists. The constant dilemma of choosing between a job or starting a business, and grappling with the notion that the grass might be greener on the other side, contributes to this perpetual cycle. The tendency to swing back and forth like a pendulum, vacillating between different aspirations, is common. Learn to embrace the simplicity of life and appreciate the straightforward path. Life becomes needlessly complex when we constantly engage in overthinking, fuelled by comparisons and external influences. Live in the present and avoid needless complications in the pursuit of a simpler, more fulfilling life.

The key lies in maintaining full alertness, and approaching every situation with complete awareness. Learn to exist in the present moment, fully engaged with your surroundings, the people around you, and the activities in which you are involved. Immerse your mind in the present actions of your body, and you will discover that happiness can be created right where you are. Individuals who cultivate awareness and practice mindfulness in various aspects of life, find themselves less entangled in life's complexities. Establish a routine where your thoughts become a product of your creation, and your mind operates according to your will.

Reflection and thought are crucial, particularly during the planning phase. However, once the plan is in motion, it is advisable to refrain from relentlessly circling it. Evaluate your track record, implement changes where needed, and rectify any mistakes in your approach. Even after these adjustments, if the outcome does not align with your target, acknowledge the influence of luck. Those adhering to the philosophy of karma, often find themselves free from unnecessary tension. Life is too short to waste your time on trivial matters. Many people invest their energy in unnecessary contemplation. Be vigilant against expending your energy on irrelevant thoughts and endeavour to lead a life, where each moment carries significance.

Actionables

- Think about it: is your mind controlling you, or are you the one directing your mind?
- Spend around ten minutes practicing full awareness—whether during mindful eating, listening, worship, meditation, or other activities.
- What kinds of thoughts lead you to overthink? Is it related to work, relationships, or decision-making?
- Analyse your thought process over the past five years—how often you thought about certain things and how much percentage of it you have achieved.

Reminders:

- Growth happens at its own pace, and sometimes it requires patience without constant interference.
- Address challenges: one step at a time, and understand that not all problems can be solved immediately.
- Life is too short to waste your time on trivial matters.
- Be vigilant against expending your energy on irrelevant thoughts, and endeavour to lead a life where each moment carries significance.

UNNECESSARY THINKING

In the previous chapter, we learned that our minds are constantly active, generating an endless stream of thoughts. There is never a pause in our thinking. We also discussed the phenomenon of overthinking, wherein an individual repeatedly thinks about a particular subject and keeps revolving around it. This practice is mentioned in religious teachings and scriptures, where it is acknowledged that thinking about the same thing repeatedly can be both positive and negative. When our thoughts are constructive and conducive to introspection, they fall under the realm of contemplation. However, when the same thought becomes a source of anxiety rather than insight, we label it as overthinking. In this chapter, we will explore the concept of unnecessary thinking.

In Hindi literature, there are three significant words: अर्थ *(arth)* or meaningful, अनर्थ (*anarth)* or meaningless, and व्यर्थ *(vyarth)* or useless. Positive thinking which carries meaning and purpose, falls under arth, where we gain something. Conversely, negative thinking falls into the category of anarth, where we only experience loss. Devoid of meaning, anarth is not vyarth but lays the groundwork for it. Anarth initiates unnecessary activities, often dominating individual actions. Unnecessary thinking occurs when thoughts persist without purpose, stirring emotions within. This leads to overthinking, which in turn fuels negative thoughts, eventually culminating in depression. Depression and stress ensue, when individuals feel they have lost everything, devoid of inner fulfilment despite external appearances. Consequently, the root cause often traces back to unnecessary thinking.

In the Jain scriptures, there is a very enlightening story about अनर्थ दंड *(anarth dand)* which illustrates the accumulation of sin through purposeless or harmful thoughts and actions. The tale features a massive crocodile named राघव मत्स्य *(Raghava matsya)*, who would eat fish to fill his stomach. Living inside his ear was a tiny fish called तंदुल मत्स्य *(Tandul matsya)*, as small as a grain of rice, yet endowed with all five senses.

When Raghava matsya slept, his mouth would remain open, allowing small fish to swim in and out freely. Although Raghava matsya stayed unaware in slumber, Tandul matsya observed everything and thought to himself: 'How foolish is this Raghava matsya! So many fish come and go, and he doesn't eat them. If I were in his place, I wouldn't let a single one escape—I would swallow them all.'

Engrossed in this contemplation, Tandul matsya remains obsessed with the crocodile's actions, pondering its thought process incessantly. However, according to Jain scriptures, this very preoccupation with observation leads Tandul matsya to a harsh fate—the seventh hell. Despite never eating a single fish, its fixation on hypothetical actions leads to its downfall; and it goes to the seventh hell and suffers punishment.

Now, the question arises: Is this punishment just or unjust? Is Tandul matsya a victim of injustice, or is there a deeper lesson to be learned? In this tale, we saw a glimpse of the consequences of unnecessary thinking—how it can trap us in a cycle of observation and speculation, deterring us from meaningful action. It prompts us to ponder the balance between contemplation and action, reminding us that while thoughts hold power, it is our deeds that shape our destiny.

The comparison to Tandul matsya raises an intriguing point about the frequency of unnecessary thinking in our lives. Indeed, countless times throughout the day, our minds engage in speculative daydreams—like the fish in the crocodile's ear.

Consider the example of the ongoing conflict between Russia and Ukraine. Upon hearing such news, a cascade of thoughts inundates our minds. We may find ourselves questioning why the conflict persists, yearning for a swift resolution to alleviate the collective tension. Yet, amidst these musings, darker thoughts may emerge—thoughts of violence, of potential solutions that involve drastic measures like bombings. While we may never act upon these thoughts, their mere presence inflicts a weight upon our conscience. Indeed, even though we are not directly involved in the conflict, our minds become battlegrounds of hypothetical scenarios and judgements. We imagine ourselves in the shoes of those embroiled in the strife, pondering how we would navigate the situation differently. Yet, these ruminations only serve to fuel our internal turmoil, exacerbating rather than alleviating the tensions we seek to escape.

So, how do we break free from this cycle of unnecessary thinking and lead more fulfilling lives? It begins with awareness—the recognition that our thoughts, though transient, hold immense power over our emotions and actions. By cultivating mindfulness, we can observe our thoughts without succumbing to their sway, allowing them to pass like clouds drifting across the sky. Furthermore, fostering empathy and understanding can temper the impulse, to judge and speculate. Instead of dwelling on hypothetical scenarios, we can channel our energies toward fostering compassion, and seeking constructive solutions to global conflicts.

Ultimately, by embracing mindfulness, empathy, and a commitment to positive action, we can transcend the confines of unnecessary thinking and strive towards a more harmonious existence, both within ourselves and in the world around us.

The stock market often triggers a flurry of thoughts and emotions within us. We reflect on past investment decisions—some yielding profits, others resulting in losses. We contemplate what could have been, imagining the potential gains if we had made different choices. Perhaps we envision ourselves with significantly larger sums, dwelling on missed opportunities and unrealised fortunes.

In the heat of these emotions, rationality often takes a backseat. We may entertain grandiose dreams of immense wealth, picturing ourselves as property moguls or stock market magnates. Yet, upon closer examination, we realise the vast chasm between aspiration and reality. Despite our desires, we may lack the financial means or expertise to execute such lofty ambitions.

However, it is crucial to recognise our limitations, and exercise caution in our financial endeavours. Blindly chasing wealth without regard for our means, can lead to financial ruin and emotional distress. Instead, we must strive for a balanced approach, grounded in realism and prudent decision-making.

By acknowledging our strengths and weaknesses, setting realistic goals, and adhering to a disciplined investment strategy, we can navigate the complexities of the financial world with confidence and resilience. In doing so, we can build a secure foundation for our future and avoid the pitfalls of reckless speculation.

Try to understand how our thoughts are generated, just like that tiny fish—Tandul matsya. Isn't it so? Everyone thought that Tandul matsya was so foolish, going to hell for nothing, and suffering. It does not happen with just a few, it happens with everyone. Now let us ask another question. Is it happening automatically, or are you consciously doing it? Is it happening intelligently, gradually becoming ingrained in your mind, or do you do it knowingly?

A person often imagines various scenarios based on emotions, and this becomes part of their thought process. A worldly person sometimes commits various sins mentally, such as, unnecessary violence. They know that this violence is unnecessary, yet they still engage in it.

Consider this scenario: someone mentions that they are dealing with insects and pests in their home, and you suggest they use pest control services. While this advice aims to help them solve their pest problem, it can also be seen as a form of violence. By reaching out to pest control on their behalf, you are assisting them in addressing the difficulties caused by pests. However, it is important to recognise that even though you did not expect anything in return, this action can still be considered a form of violence.

Why is that? Why burden yourself with the potential for sin? If you are acting out of concern for the safety and security of your own home, that is one thing. But if you intervene in your neighbour's affairs unnecessarily, you may be unnecessarily taking on a burden of wrongdoing. It might be more appropriate, to let your neighbour handle the issue. To avoid perpetuating violence, it is crucial to understand our thoughts, emotions, and actions. By striving to take positive and peaceful actions, we can minimise harm and contribute to a more harmonious environment for everyone involved.

When friends face pest infestations, our instinct to help is natural. However, it is vital to weigh in our assistance against their autonomy, and the broader consequences. While supporting them in addressing the issue is important, imposing solutions without their input may cause unintended harm. Striking a balance between aid and respect ensures compassionate support; without infringing on their choices.

Now, let us look at an example: a couple is travelling on a train with a young child. If you encounter them sitting nearby, and their son appears to be five or six years old, what would you suggest? Given that you are not related to them and just happened to meet them on the train, they ask you whether they should buy a ticket for the child or not. What would you say? You might suggest they should buy the ticket based on the child's apparent age, even if they claim he is only four but appears to be six. If they ask whether they should buy the ticket, let them decide. It is up to them to buy the ticket or not. But if you let them continue without buying the ticket, until the child's height increases and he appears older; you have indirectly taught them to cheat. Now, what was there for you to gain from this? You are not receiving any money from them; the money for the child's ticket would not be going to you.

The feeling of jealousy often arises from our insecurities, rather than any hindrance to others progress. Others advance based on their abilities and opportunities, not because of our jealousy. Instead of feeling jealous, we should celebrate their progress, offer praise, and acknowledge their achievements. Jealousy only brings suffering to ourselves and does not harm anyone else in the process.

Indulging in unnecessary sin can harm you, even if you lead a life free from obligations to others. Much of our time is spent on unnecessary thinking, which we strive to avoid. The key to overcoming this lies in mindful living. Practicing mindfulness daily, even in simple activities like eating or worshipping, can help. By staying fully present and aware in each moment, you can rise above futile activities and unnecessary sins. This practice showcases high intellect and social awareness, ultimately leading to self-preservation, which is paramount in life.

Instead of dwelling on unnecessary thoughts, everyone must take a moment to sit peacefully and contemplate. Have you ever analysed how much time we spend on unnecessary activities in our daily routines? How much time is devoted to unnecessary thinking?

It is essential to reflect on this aspect of our lives. While it is natural to analyse everything and think about others, it is equally important to introspect and consider where our own time is spent, and where it is wasted. Whether it is at the temple, in the office, in the kitchen, while watching TV, reading the newspaper, watching movies or series, talking to someone, or giving suggestions to someone, it is worth evaluating how much time we allocate to these activities.

Actionables

Contemplate:

- How much time do we spend in our daily routine on unnecessary thinking?
- How much time are you spending on unnecessary activities? Whether it is at the temple, in the office, in the kitchen, while watching TV, reading the newspaper, watching movies or series, talking to someone, or giving suggestions to someone.

Reminders:

- Every person lives like the Tandul matsya, the tiny fish, and engages in unnecessary thinking.
- The feeling of jealousy arises unnecessarily from your insecurity; it does not hold back the progress of others.

POSITIVE AND NEGATIVE THINKING

Our thoughts have a substantial impact on shaping our lives, whether for the better or worse. They influence our speech and behaviour, guiding our actions even when we try to act differently. Unlike physical activity and speech, our thoughts persist continuously. Our worldview and beliefs strongly shape our behaviour. We carefully consider our words before speaking, and plan our actions accordingly. Our thoughts are susceptible to both positive and negative influences.

In cities, you will find both garbage dumps and gardens. People naturally gravitate towards green spaces for a positive start to their day, while avoiding garbage dumps. Just as we prioritise keeping our physical surroundings clean, it is equally important to address the garbage in our minds. Negative thoughts have the power to influence our behaviour and outlook. To maintain a healthy mindset, we must learn to recognise and discard these negative thoughts. Similarly, engaging in gossip and negativity allows mental garbage to accumulate, ultimately affecting our overall perspective on life. Therefore, it is crucial to actively reject negativity and nurture a positive mindset for our overall well-being.

A pessimist tends to perceive difficulty in every opportunity, while an optimist discovers opportunity in every difficulty. Pessimism fixates on trouble even in favourable circumstances, whereas optimism seeks opportunity amidst challenges. Do you often anticipate the worst in good situations? When encountering something new, do you question your abilities or seek ways to improve? Negative thoughts concentrate on potential failures and doubts, while positive thoughts explore possibilities for enhancement. Instead of immediately seeking solutions, pessimists often ruminate on problems and obstacles.

When we start believing something is too difficult, excuses and doubts take root, impeding progress. Conversely, when we believe something is achievable, our minds shift towards finding solutions and strategies to make it happen, regardless of initial difficulties.

We all aspire to progress and embark on new endeavours in life. It is crucial to be vigilant of our initial thoughts, ensuring they don't incline towards negativity. Adhering to this principle and embracing positivity is key to achieving success. When negativity is our first response, our mind works to validate it, consuming our energy to prove it right. Conversely, when our initial intuition is positive, our brain directs its energy toward validating it in a positive direction.

Therefore, it is vital to prevent our initial thoughts from turning negative. The first word we utter should always be positive. Practice affirming statements like, 'I can achieve this easily. It is not difficult. It is quite manageable.' If others can succeed, why can't we? If ordinary people can accomplish it, why not us?

Our first words often echo negativity: 'The obstacles are immense.' This mental journey is about exploring pathways; indeed, here lies a blockade. If we tread this path, we will encounter obstacles. Focusing solely on these hurdles blinds us to anything else. Conversely, a mindset filled with positivity, will find a way even amidst roadblocks. An optimist sees one night between two days, while a pessimist sees one day between two nights.

Hearing about major companies undergoing mass layoffs can trigger worries about one's job security. People may fear phrases like, 'What if I'm next?' For those with a positive outlook, even if a company with a workforce of 300,000 reduces its staff by 30,000, there is still a significant workforce of 270,000 remaining. In such a scenario, the initial focus might be on the majority still employed rather than the minority laid off.

In management, a small group at the top level makes key decisions and long-term plans, while the lower levels of the hierarchy consist of a larger number of individuals. This structure resembles a pyramid, with a few at the top and many at the bottom. In the Indian economy, for example, 5 per cent of the population holds 95 per cent of the wealth due to their unique perspective. They consistently focus on the positive, seeing opportunities where others see obstacles. Conversely, those at the bottom often perceive only darkness and failure, even in the simplest tasks. Their negative outlook influences their experiences and shapes their reality.

When we encounter someone who always focuses on negativity, it is crucial to avoid them, recognising as they aim to dump their negative thoughts onto others. Associating with them, risks absorbing their pessimism. It is like allowing ourselves to become containers for their emotional garbage. Conversely, meeting someone who consistently shares positivity is like receiving a bouquet, filling us with fragrance.

Most people tend to dwell on negativity, which reflects what they carry inside. Those who speak kindly and positively harbour goodness within them, maintaining an optimistic outlook on life. Conversely, individuals who spread fear and negativity, internally harbour such thoughts and are unlikely to find success in any aspect of life. Despite short-term achievements, they remain unfulfilled, plagued by unhappiness and perpetual troubles.

Believing in ourselves and our abilities is essential regardless of our background or circumstances. Our financial situation, upbringing, or education level should not constrain our aspirations. Instead, we should strive to exceed these limitations, and pursue our dreams with determination. Blaming others for our failures is simple, but taking responsibility for our actions is the first step toward personal growth. As we progress, let's remember that our mindset and attitude significantly influence our reality.

By embracing positivity and resilience, we can overcome challenges and attain success in life.

Consider this example: During a seminar, a motivational speaker used a bucket and bricks to demonstrate a powerful lesson. Initially, he filled the bucket with bricks, leaving some space. Then, he added small brick pieces and sand until the bucket was full. Despite doubts, the demonstration showed that creative thinking always finds room for more. This highlighted the importance of maintaining a positive mindset and exploring all possibilities, even in tight situations. The speaker then challenged the audience by asking if the bucket was empty or full and poured water into it. He further sprayed some fragrance on it. This illustrated that even when things seem impossible, there's always room for more. This mirrors life's situations, where initially, there may seem to be no solution but exploring all possibilities reveals hidden potential.

The key to success lies in changing your mindset, not the situation itself. Despite facing the same circumstances, what sets extraordinary individuals apart, particularly leaders, is their mindset. They are ordinary people who approach challenges with a different perspective.

Consider seeking a job. What is the initial thought that comes to mind? It might be, 'I've been rejected thrice already, what now? I'll probably get rejected again.' This negative thought pattern dictates subsequent actions, leading to a cycle of disappointment. Instead, why not think, 'How can I improve? How can I approach this differently?' Embracing proactive mindset shifts focus, towards finding solutions rather than dwelling on setbacks. It is essential to break free from the confines of negativity and aspire for higher levels of achievement, rather than remaining stagnant—at the bottom of the pyramid amidst the crowd.

The initial thought that arises, is often driven by our subconscious mind, which tends to lean towards optimism. However, at a conscious level, our thoughts may differ. It is crucial to address and challenge these subconscious patterns.

Reflect on your reactions to minor inconveniences, like a delayed breakfast or newspaper. Do you immediately become irritated? This reflects where your mindset currently stands. It is essential to work towards changing these reactions. Even in minor incidents, we tend to belittle ourselves. For example, getting a flat tire while driving might lead to thoughts like, 'Nothing ever works out for me. I'll never make it on time.' Instead, we should strive to encourage ourselves in such situations and recognise the potential within us, even with the smallest events.

Whenever you feel like there is nothing left in life, remember that there are still numerous possibilities awaiting you. Believe in these possibilities and keep moving forward. Remember, where we place a period, that signifies the end of a sentence. But what happens when we see three dots (ellipsis), it signifies that the game is not over; there is more to unfold. Even in moments of defeat, it is crucial to remember that it is not the end—every attempt matters. While your initial intuition may lean towards negativity, it does not dictate your entire journey. It is saddening when negativity becomes so overwhelming, that suicidal thoughts arise.

In a jungle, a group of small rabbits gathered, appearing tired and defeated. One rabbit lamented about the fragility of their lives, fearing being crushed or eaten at any moment. Another mentioned the threat of humans capturing and consuming them. Yet another rabbit expressed hopelessness, feeling unable to escape from anyone. However, an elder rabbit intervened, urging them to pause and observe. They noticed a group of frogs nearby, even more frightened than themselves, desperately jumping into the water to evade danger. This sight made the rabbits realise they were not alone in their fears. With this new perspective, they felt stronger and more resilient, and soon they began playing happily in the jungle again.

The story carries a profound message: When life feels devoid of hope and filled with sorrow, it is easy to believe that death is the only way out. When we are faced with criticism and ridicule, they overshadow any sense of appreciation, thereby fuelling feelings of worthlessness and despair. However, upon reflection we realise, that many others face far worse circumstances than us, yet lead much more fulfilling lives.

Transforming negative thoughts into positive ones is the key. With determination and a positive mindset, we can navigate life's obstacles and emerge stronger than before. Controlling our initial thoughts is crucial. Our first impulse should never be negative, and our first word should not be, no or impossible. Even the word impossible, itself suggests that, I'm possible. When we feel like something is impossible, we must remember that every impossibility hides a possibility within it.

However, we often add I'm to possible, turning it into impossible and making everything seem unattainable. Yet, every question mark holds an answer, and every situation has potential. Even when it seems as if there is no way forward, we must sit calmly and reflect. From impossibility, possibilities emerge offering new pathways. Even in the face of rejection or setbacks, we must remain calm and persistent. Surrounding ourselves with positive influences and absorbing their stories and thoughts, can help shift our mindset toward positivity. By aligning ourselves with positivity, our thoughts gradually become more optimistic.

Maintaining a positive attitude can make a significant difference in our outcomes. When we approach challenges with a negative mindset, we are already setting ourselves up for failure. However, by shifting our initial thoughts towards positivity, we open ourselves up to possibilities and opportunities.

Even if the outcome is rejection or failure, approaching it with a positive mindset allows us to learn and grow from the experience. We have nothing to lose by adopting a positive outlook. Patience is the key in this process, as it allows us to see opportunities that we may have overlooked, in our haste or pessimism. Just like the bucket filled with water, there's always room for more. Even when it seems like there is no space left, a positive mindset can create room for new possibilities. Seeking guidance from experienced and successful individuals, can also help illuminate new paths forward. Ultimately, embracing positivity and seeking out mentors can lead us toward success and fulfilment.

Actionables

- Recall incidents when things went wrong, such as losses in relationships. What was your initial reaction, and what was the outcome?
- Reflect on the moments in your life, where you felt like there was nothing left. How did you overcome them and what was the learning point?
- Engage in light stretching or deep breathing exercises to centre the mind and body, preparing for the day's challenges.

Reminders:

- It is crucial to be vigilant of our initial thoughts, ensuring they do not incline towards negativity.
- The first word we utter should always be positive.
- Beginning with positive words of encouragement and thoughts of gratitude, establishes a foundation for success.
- Remember, even amidst thorns, a rose blooms, spreading beauty and fragrance. What do you see in life—roses or thorns?

OVERCOMING JEALOUSY

THIS CHAPTER EXPLORES THE CONCEPT OF JEALOUSY: its origins, its impact, and ways to protect ourselves from it. Why does jealousy arise? What causes these feelings? How does jealousy affect us negatively? Consider why the thought, 'Why do others have more, while I have less?' emerges. Is it because you struggle to accept others success? Jealousy often involves resentment towards others growth. Is this feeling automatic? If jealousy were natural, wouldn't everyone experience it? Yet, many people are unaffected by it, and some even use it positively, while most harm themselves by comparing themselves with others. Reflect on, when and towards whom you feel jealous. Does jealousy always occur, or only occasionally?

The entire world notices others, and people do see each other, but why does the feeling arise that you cannot digest someone else's progress? They are progressing through their hard work and making significant, rapid progress. Why do such emotions develop, making it difficult for you to accept their success? What is the root cause of this? It is understandable that when you cannot tolerate others progress, a person starts to feel envious. This is what happens in jealousy, but why does it happen and particularly, with whom does it occur?

Jealousy can arise in various situations, there is one situation where your growth is not happening, but someone else is progressing, and you cannot accept it. Then there is another situation where both people are growing simultaneously, yet you still cannot accept it. For example, someone who excels at work might notice their colleagues envy despite everyone receiving promotions. This emotion is not confined to professional settings; it can also appear among close family members, such as sisters-in-law, mothers and daughters, or siblings.

Even within families, one person's success can spark jealousy in another. For instance, a daughter might envy her mother's beauty, or sisters-in-law might feel resentment if one of them achieves more than the other. Jealousy can also occur in religious settings. In temples, for instance, people might feel envious if one individual receives more attention than another. This emotion is pervasive and can affect everyone, regardless of their status or education including monks.

Now, consider a deeper question: Is jealousy always relative, or can it be absolute? Is it necessary for someone else to be present for jealousy to occur? This is a profound thought worth reflecting on. Is it possible to experience jealousy when there is no one around; when you have not met anyone, and there is no competition? Who would you feel jealous of? Is someone necessary for you to feel envy, or can it happen without anyone else? Does jealousy always arise from comparison with others, or can it occur on its own, without anyone else being involved? When it comes to jealousy, it is relative. However, there is another aspect to consider. Every coin has two sides. On one side, there is jealousy, and on the opposite side is self-praise. A person who desires self-praise can never truly escape jealousy.

Jealousy is often understood as the inability to accept someone else's success. When others progress and we struggle to accept it, we may feel jealousy. However, the root cause of jealousy lies in the desire for self-praise. Imagine putting effort into something like preparing a meal or working hard, but receiving no recognition or appreciation. How would that affect you emotionally? Would you remain indifferent, or would you long for recognition and blessings? If you find it difficult to be at ease without this acknowledgement, it reveals a desire for self-praise, which can further lead to jealousy.

Both jealousy and the need for self-praise, make people outward-focused, hindering introspection. True wisdom involves not seeking external validation, yet, many fall into the trap of craving praise for even minor actions performed. This desire for recognition is not just human nature; it is a deeper issue that drives our emotional responses and behaviour. The more outward-focused a person is, the stronger their craving for recognition becomes. In contrast, those who are inward-focused remain unaffected by external validation, as their achievements are for their own satisfaction.

Even in spiritual practices or good deeds, it is natural to notice if others are watching. To reduce jealousy and the need for praise, cultivating an inward-focused mindset is essential. Although, it is challenging due to the presence of constant social interactions, striving for this perspective can help manage these desires.

Jealousy and self-praise bring numerous negative consequences as well. When we are jealous, we harm ourselves. A jealous person can never be creative, as their energy is drained by envy. As jealousy intensifies, it often leads to destructive behaviours like backbiting, spreading negativity, and even attempting to bring others down. This cycle can escalate from jealousy to gossip, and in extreme cases, to actions aimed at harming others. Acharya Shree Vidya Sagar Ji Maharaj says that there is a principle: 'Criticising others while praising oneself; covering up the virtues of others while trying to showcase one's own, leads a person downward.' He identifies it as one of the primary reasons for a person's downfall.

Let me share a memorable story about two students. One was always the top student consistently coming first in class, while the other always came second. The second student could not tolerate the top student's success. As exams approached, he decided to sabotage the top student by hiding his notes. At the last moment, the top student realised his notes were missing, which affected his performance. However, the student who took the notes ended up suffering more. He fell into a deep depression and struggled academically in the following class. Despite visits to doctors, his condition remained a mystery until he finally confessed what he had done. He apologised to the top student and returned the notes. Only then did he find inner peace and begin to recover.

The principle of karma states, that when a person filled with jealousy starts engaging in certain actions, it creates obstacles and disruptions in their life. They end up suffering from these consequences in the future as well. The biggest internal factor that brings a person down is jealousy. Therefore, jealousy not only causes problems in the present but also brings adverse effects in the future. No one intends to be jealous, but it still occurs. So, how can we avoid jealousy? What should be done?

The humbler and more modest you become, the more your focus shifts inward rather than outward. This humility naturally reduces jealousy. While not everyone can easily become introspective, developing humility helps. As you grow humbler, you start seeing virtues in others instead of flaws. This change in perspective transforms those who are improving into sources of inspiration rather than jealousy. By embracing humility and recognising the good in others, jealousy diminishes. The simplest way to overcome jealousy is to rise above self-praise and cultivate humility. As you develop these qualities and learn to be at ease, you will begin to see only goodness in the world around you.

One more question: Do you engage in gossip? Do you speak ill of others? Or do you simply enjoy hearing gossip more than speaking it yourself? Gossip, too, begins with jealousy; it cannot exist without it.

There is a great example involving Socrates, the philosopher. One day, a student rushed to him, excited to share some gossip about someone in the marketplace. As he started to speak, Socrates stopped him and asked, 'Before you tell me anything, tell me if what you're going to say is positive, negative, or neither?' The student replied that it was negative. Socrates then asked, 'Is it something you've seen with your own eyes or just something you've heard?' The student said that he had not seen it himself, but that it was widely discussed in the market. Socrates told him that if it was neither something good, nor seen firsthand, nor useful, then he did not need to hear it. He said listening to such things was like having garbage that only spreads dirt. Socrates emphasised that if the information is not good, true, or useful, it does not benefit anyone.

People who indulge in jealousy, self-praise, and gossip lose more than they gain. They fill themselves with negativity, and end up with nothing but emptiness. Socrates encouraged the practice of self-awareness, humility, and focusing on positive and useful information. If you avoid these negative tendencies and embrace humility and constructive actions, you will overcome jealousy and find more satisfaction in life. If not, you may feel bored and dissatisfied, lacking the zest for life. Understanding this is crucial for personal growth and fulfilment. Introspect, analyse yourself, and focus on your own growth rather than others.

Actionables

Reflect on these questions and try to introspect.

- Have you ever felt jealous?
- When do you start feeling a sense of jealousy?
- Who do you feel jealous of?
- Where does jealousy arise?
- Why does it occur?
- What triggers these emotions?
- Does jealousy always occur, or only occasionally?

Reminders:

- By cultivating self-awareness, practicing gratitude, seeking inspiration, and focusing on personal growth, you can protect yourself from jealousy and create a more fulfilling and contented life.
- Criticising others while praising oneself, covering up the virtues of others while trying to showcase one's own, leads a person downward.
- People who indulge in jealousy, self-praise, and gossip lose more than they gain.

DETACHED ATTACHMENT

We often contemplate various ways to bring happiness into our lives. Despite unlimited desires, achieving desired results remains rare. Why is it so rare that we cannot obtain what we desire? If the expected results are not obtained, we should look within ourselves to see where the deficiency lies. We have been trying to understand which paths lead us to happiness, and what roadblocks hinder our progress.

We explored various reasons and solutions to comprehend the right path, overcoming ignorance and desires that often trap us. Further, self-reflection—is a powerful tool—alongside activities focused on mindfulness and meditation techniques, which help us reach our goals. Success in any endeavour requires mental but also verbal and physical involvement. As the verse in the Bhagavad Gita suggests, 'Focus on action rather than the outcome.' True happiness can be achieved through our actions. It is a crucial question to ask ourselves: do we undertake any actions in our lives without expecting outcomes?

Let us comprehend this concept with a compelling story. A fifteen-year-old boy goes to a guru and expresses his desire to learn swordsmanship. The boy asks the guru, how many years of hard work it will take for him to become an expert in swordsmanship. The guru carefully observes the boy's eagerness, and says that if he practices as instructed, he will become an expert in five years. The boy finds five years too long and seeks a shortcut, asking if there is a way to learn faster. He pledges to put in extra effort and work diligently. The guru then estimates, it will take him ten years even if he doubles his efforts. Confused, the boy questions why the timeframe has doubled, when he intended to work harder. The boy asked for a shortcut to learn speedily; the reason being his elderly parents at home. Despite promising hard work, sleepless nights, and being completely honest, the guru told him it would take twenty-five years now.

The guru explains, that rushing and overexerting oneself never leads to success; rather, wastes one's energy. He emphasises the importance of being deeply engaged in the process without being attached to the outcome. The guru's teachings help the boy understand that true mastery comes from dedication to the process, not from seeking quick results.

When students take exams, their focus may be on performing well or getting good results. Did you know, that anxiety about results can affect performance negatively. Most students who score in the 95-97 per cent range, often fall just short of reaching the cutoff of 98-99 per cent.

Why does this happen? They get overwhelmed by umpteen worries about what they should have done, what could happen, or what will not. We must be solely devoted to the process, forgetting about whether it will happen or not, how it will happen, where we will end up, which college or branch we'll get, or whether we'll get it at all. Likewise, in interviews, some people might concentrate solely on getting a high-paying job offer, but this attitude could hold back their performance. Those who forget about the results, and focus on the process tend to perform better.

The student who remains completely relaxed, is the one who can perform the best. However, when doubts start creeping into our minds whether it will happen or not, our performance suffers as a result. Many students excel in preparatory exams like weekly tests and mock exams during coaching classes, but falter in the final exam. Why does this happen? What is the reason? Often, the answer lies in examination anxiety—the mental and emotional turmoil that builds up under high pressure, fear of failure, and the burden of expectations.

In India, this pressure is particularly intense. Entrance exams like NEET, JEE, UPSC, and others are viewed as life-defining events. The competition is fierce, and the societal narrative often equates exam success with future success, amplifying the stress manifold. As a result, even students who are thoroughly prepared may experience racing thoughts, self-doubt, memory blocks, or even physical symptoms like sweating, nausea, or dizziness just before or during the exam. This mental clutter clouds their ability to think clearly and perform effectively.

A person who has nothing to lose always performs better. In competitive exams, most students who pass are usually those who attempt the exam for the first or second time because they have less stress at that time. They are always prepared for the worst-case scenario. Their backup mind is ready to accept whatever happens—whether they will be selected or not. So, they relax and do not stay stressed. When fear disappears, all our energy will start channelling in the proper direction in the process.

The former Indian Cricket Team captain, M.S. Dhoni used to be known as Captain Cool. Why? He always performed well in the last moments and never lost his calm during the matches no matter how bad the situation was. He would come in at the sixth or seventh number and still perform well. Why? Because he had nothing to lose. Hence, all his energy was directed towards productive performance.

In cricket matches, many players experience what is called the nervous 90. When a player is playing exceptionally well, hitting boundaries like sixes and fours with ease, what happens when they reach the 90-run mark? Typically, these top players, who were performing brilliantly, suddenly feel the pressure and struggle to maintain their momentum when nearing a century. What starts going on in their minds? Will they make a century or not? They become very cautious, fearing they might make a mistake and get out. The thought process begins: 'I don't want to make a mistake.' While this thought process starts, they get out. Look at the history of even the top players; check how many times they have become victims of the nervous 90.

In states of contemplation, there is no tension, no anxiety, and motivation comes from within. Discussing the importance of setting high goals, expressing the desire for happiness, visualising, reading about it, and talking about it—all of these are essential to motivate us to give our best, 110 per cent, on the path. Understanding this invokes a sense of devotion, making it crucial to have. Focusing on raising the goal is essential for personal satisfaction. However, while motivation pushes us towards complete devotion, it is equally crucial to understand how the results will unfold. Many get stuck here, failing to take action or faltering at the brink of success.

Why do we fail to deliver our 100 per cent in our process, and our paths? It is because attachment, which brings eagerness, also leads to detriment. Individuals get trapped in it. Whether you look at a student's life, a professional's life, a woman's life, or even a child's life, you'll find people getting stuck at a certain point. They may have different goals, but many still struggle. We're talking about balancing attachment and detachment. Attachment comes from the process and the path, while detachment comes from the outcome and the destination.

So, what should happen? We should focus on our journey, and on the paths, we are taking. If we are following the right path, and doing our tasks correctly as instructed, the results will naturally turn out well. There is no need to worry excessively about the outcome. People often get stuck, worrying about the result instead of focusing on the journey. You only have control over your actions, not the desire for the result. Initial expectations are natural because they drive our actions, but we should not dwell on planning indefinitely. Once we have a plan, we should focus on executing it to achieve our goals.

Ultimately, we all seek happiness, so why should we get caught up in unnecessary concerns? Joy comes when a person is completely tension-free and stays on their path. Expecting certain outcomes, like children caring for their parents in old age, or taking them on an annual pilgrimage can lead to sorrow if unmet. Instead, focus on performing duties with utmost devotion and detachment from the outcome. Give your duty 100 per cent commitment and devotion, but let go of the expectations you have for achieving specific results. Embracing this mindset helps avoid unnecessary sorrow, and fosters a healthier approach to life's outcomes. When we are putting in the effort, there comes a point where things are beyond our control. At that moment, it is best to let go of whatever has happened. Your expectations are a part of your path, not your destination.

The concept of performing actions without the desire for results is not incorrectly stated. The scriptures stress on the importance of performing actions without any attachment to the results—and even discourage the desire for liberation. Liberation manifests when one deeply engages in the process, walks the path, and eventually renounces the world through meditation. Success comes to those who are devoted to the process, free from distractions. Overthinking and worry can derail progress. So, focusing on the present moment is crucial for achieving success without unnecessary stress.

Actionables

- Recall the moments of your life, where you were unsuccessful and analyse why this happened to you?
- Everyone wants happiness, but do you want the path to happiness?
- Everyone desires liberation, but reflect on whether you desire the path to liberation, or the idea of liberation?
- What happens in real life? Are your expectations focused on the journey or the destination?

Reminders:

- Focus on actions you perform, rather than the outcome.
- True mastery comes from dedication to the process, not from seeking quick results.
- As much as we desire the destination, it is equally important to desire the path.
- The person who desires happiness internally, will not look at the result; they will always focus on the process or path.

PART 4

COMMUNICATION AND RELATIONSHIPS

NONVIOLENT COMMUNICATION (NVC)

COMMUNICATION IS AN INCREDIBLY POWERFUL TOOL; it can either elevate the society or bring it down. There are two sides to communication: one that promotes violence, and another that promotes peace. Words have the power to hurt just as much as physical violence, sometimes even more. While physical violence usually affects specific people or groups, harmful words can resonate globally. For instance, the impact of a gunshot or explosion is confined, but words spoken once can reach and affect everyone. Throughout history, influential people have made statements that changed the course of nations. This demonstrates that communication can be a force for good, driving progress, or a source of discord and confusion.

How we communicate significantly influences our behaviour. It is crucial to be mindful of how we express ourselves. Our communication should strive to be nonviolent, ensuring our words do not harm others but promote their progress. Indeed, words hold immense power.

Let us explore what constitutes violent communication. What behaviours fall under this category? When and with whom do we use it? What circumstances trigger its use? Can we identify elements in our communication that might negatively impact others? Understanding this concept is vital. Often, people speak thoughtlessly but at times, things are said with the intent to harm. In religious teachings, even monks and ascetics, known for their dedication to nonviolence and goodwill towards all beings, are urged to employ gentle, pleasant language and communicate with thoughtful care and compassion.

Violent communication is not just about physical harm; it is also about the impact of words on others. Consider history: the Mahabharata's beginning was triggered by Draupadi's words to Duryodhana: 'Blind son of a blind man.' This single sentence sparked widespread destruction and death. Can one sentence cause so much harm? In the same epic, Yudhishthira's words, 'Ashwatthama is dead,' led to Dronacharya surrendering. Were those words true or false? They were partly true. While an elephant named Ashwatthama was indeed killed, Dronacharya only heard the part about Ashwatthama being dead, which brought about his surrender and fuelled violence.

Have you ever thought about how you use your words in your day-to-day life? There are four styles of narration:

- प्रथमानुयोग *(Prathamanuyog)*

- चरणानुयोग *(Charananuyog)*
- करुणानुयोग *(Karunanuyog)*
- द्रव्यानुयोग *(Dravyanuyog)*

These four approaches can be applied in practical life to understand how essential effective communication is and how it functions.

Let us learn, the difference between violent and nonviolent communication through an example. When a child falls and starts crying, a mother responds in two ways: through violent and nonviolent modes of communication.

In a nonviolent approach, she might follow different methods. According to prathamanuyog, she gives examples of great personalities, telling the child how they lived without falling and played without getting hurt. In the charananuyog approach, she offers practical advice, such as, 'If you watch where you are going, you won't fall.' Using karunanuyog, she might say, 'You must have done something wrong yesterday, which is why you got hurt today.' Through the dravyanuyog approach, she reassures the child by saying, 'It is nothing; you are a brave boy. It's just a small scratch on your knee, not your soul.'

Conversely, in violent communication, the mother's responses are harsher. In prathamanuyog, she might compare and say, 'Your brother walks so well, while you are so careless,' which injures the child's self-esteem. Following charananuyog, she might scold, 'Can't you see where you're going? Are you blind?' hurting the child's feelings. According to karunanuyog, she blames the child, 'You lied yesterday, didn't you? That's why you fell today.'

Lastly, in dravyanuyog, she criticises, 'You can't do anything right; you're always falling.'

Analyse yourself. Is your sentence motivating or demotivating the other person? If we understand these nonviolent communication methods, life can become beautiful like heaven. If not, it can create a living hell. How do you communicate with people you spend your life with, especially your children? How do you deliver your words? If your words demotivate your child, understand that this is violent communication.

Now, let us consider a situation, where truth is spoken harshly. Parents often say, 'You're a fool,' or that 'You have no calibre.' If a child hears these words repeatedly, what message does he internalise from his parents? Even if the child is weak in studies, or simply lacks the knowledge, practice or skills required to be better, what impact does your sentence have on their subconscious mind? It becomes ingrained in their minds. They think, if my parents are saying so, it must be true—'I must be a fool.' As you speak the truth harshly, you inflict mental violence creating a negative mindset. Instead of identifying and addressing the underlying reasons for their poor performance, these negative affirmations damage the child's potential and self-belief. This is violent communication because it causes lasting mental and emotional harm. The biggest form of violent communication is when you cause mental harm.

Scriptures identify various types of violent communication, including words which are: harsh, cruel, mocking, angry, quarrelsome, violence-inducing, hostility-inducing, sarcastic, and defamatory along with gossip and meaningless talk. These forms of speech are harmful and should be avoided. It is important to be mindful of our language and promote kindness, understanding, and support in our interactions.

Spreading rumours or negative talk about others is harmful. Almost everyone criticises others often out of jealousy. When we point out someone's mistakes to others, even if true, it damages reputations and shatters peace of mind. Criticism will not help or change someone. To support, uplift, or change someone's heart, we must avoid criticism and approach them with understanding and compassion.

A story appears in Jain philosophy. A thief once posed as a monk and came to the house of a wealthy merchant. The merchant had built a very beautiful temple in his home. The merchant had to go out of town for business purposes for eight days, so, he entrusted the monk with the task of taking care of the temple. However, the monk who had come to steal, saw the opportunity to steal the valuable gold and silver idols from the temple. As soon as the merchant left, the monk stole everything and absconded. The soldiers saw the monk running away with the stolen goods and tried to catch him. When the merchant returned, he asked the soldiers why they were trying to catch him. The soldiers replied that he had stolen the valuable gold and silver idols from the temple. The merchant said, 'No, I had instructed him to bring those idols to me.' Hearing this, the monk, a thief, fell at the feet of the merchant. He admitted, 'You saved me. You knew I had stolen, yet you did not accuse me of wrongdoing.' From that day on, he took a vow to not commit any misconduct. If we want to change someone, lift them and support them; as criticism will never bring about that change.

Now, consider two scenarios: one where someone is doing something wrong and we need to ensure their safety, and another where we have no connection to the person but still criticise them. In 99 per cent of cases, you start speaking ill about someone with whom you have nothing to do; so, what do you gain?

Sarcastic and hurtful comments can also be a form of violence-causing emotional, mental, or social harm. Many people, intentionally or unintentionally, engage in such negative communication instead of offering compliments. If we want to reform someone, then instead of bashing them publicly, we should tell their mentors whom they respect; who are in their best interest, or their parents. It should not be done sarcastically, with irony, or by belittling them. The result can only be achieved through much politeness. It is necessary to instil trust in the person we are dealing with. Without it, it is not possible.

Ego and arrogance in our communication aim to belittle others and elevate oneself. Demeaning language, such as addressing someone diminutively is prevalent, especially in competitive environments like the workplace. In contrast, individuals with inner richness and quality speak humbly, as their tone reflects their character. For instance, Abraham Lincoln, despite being the 16th President of the United States, would bow and greet others respectfully. When asked why, he explained that he did this not for the sake of others, but because it reflected his qualities. Similarly, using harsh language degrades oneself, as it causes personal downfall.

Until now, we have discussed bringing someone down and portraying them negatively, as forms of violent communication. Now, let us understand self-violent communication. When a person becomes eager for self-praise, they begin to expect it from others. On a micro level, this too is a form of violence. As soon as we start desiring self-praise, our growth halts. We can no longer progress because the words of praise and the desire to hear them inflate our ego. This hinders our ability to perform well and stay creative. Ultimately, we begin committing violence against ourselves.

Further, jealousy is a significant medium for violent communication. When you envy someone and start criticising them, even in the desire for self-praise, somewhere there is hidden jealousy indirectly. When we think 'I am great', the other side of the coin automatically emerges that the other person is small. If I should receive praise, it means pushing others down. That is why self-praise is considered dangerous.

In short, violent communication is when your words hurt, demotivate, or demean the other person, causing psychological or emotional harm. It can be as damaging as physical violence, sometimes even more so, because words have a lasting impact. Therefore, it is essential to be mindful of how we communicate, especially with our loved ones.

Actionables

- Self-analyse the people you meet daily, whether they are your family members, colleagues, society members, relatives, or distant relatives—how do you communicate with them in your day-to-day life?
- In real life, when you observe someone delivering a sentence in a particular way, how do you identify the positive or negative? What thoughts cross your mind about that person?

Reminders:

- Violent communication means any form of communication that discourages, demotivates, or hurts the other person emotionally or mentally.
- It is not just about physical violence, but also the impact of your words on the other person's feelings and mindset.
- In contrast, nonviolent communication compliments the person for their efforts, encourages them, and supports their positive changes.
- When you see someone trying to improve and do good, your response should be uplifting and supportive rather than sarcastic and critical.

NONVIOLENT THINKING (NVT)

In the previous chapter, we explored two types of communication: violent and nonviolent. While one can escalate conflicts, the other adopts peace. Words have a powerful impact, sometimes hurting more than physical harm. We discussed the signs of violent communication, like harsh words, cruelty, defamation, or excessive teasing, which can lead to conflicts. Even small words can deeply wound someone, shattering their spirit and causing them to lose hope. In this chapter, let us learn how we can shift from violent communication to a kinder, nonviolent approach.

Violent communication starts with our violent thought process, while nonviolent communication begins with our nonviolent thinking. To achieve nonviolent communication, we must first understand our thought process. Are our thoughts violent or nonviolent? The thoughts we generate influence our words. What we think is often based on what we read, what we hear from others, and our learning and understanding. Our thought process is not necessarily fixed. When we find a good mentor or a positive personality who understands and guides us well, our thinking can become positive.

Nonviolent thinking is essential to nonviolent communication. Therefore, before we speak to anyone, we should learn to observe ourselves, read our thoughts, and change our mindset. There is a well-known saying, 'Weigh your words before you speak.' Do words have a weight that needs to be measured? Do words have a value that needs to be appraised? Indeed, words carry significant meaning. Thus, we should weigh our words before we speak and understand their value. This practice begins with our nonviolent thinking. Once we refine, improve, and organise our thoughts, our speech will naturally transform. As our words change, our habits and behaviour will change, which will influence our environment and the people around us.

We often blame others or our surroundings for mistreatment, particularly those we spend the most time with: partners, colleagues, or family members. Analyse your daily interactions: most are with these close individuals, yet communication with occasional acquaintances tends to be better. This is because we often take those we see daily, for granted, leading to misunderstandings and unexpressed emotions. Minor unexpressed thoughts and feelings can build up, causing issues. However, a bit of self-reflection and small internal changes can significantly improve our relationships and overall happiness. Everyone desires good relationships and a joyful life, but we often fail to achieve this and blame others instead. By reflecting on ourselves and improving our communication, we can start to see positive changes.

To cultivate good thoughts, deliberate the company you keep and the nature of your interactions. Are the people around you discussing positive, honest, and compassionate ideas that bring you happiness? Evaluate the quality of your conversations, especially including those on your mobile phone. Are they morally enriching and fruitful? Great minds discuss ideas, focusing on societal improvement and innovation. Average minds discuss events, often lacking substance. Small minds gossip about people. Many people engage in superficial discussions about politics, entertainment, and gossip. They endlessly talk about politics, cinema, sports, and ongoing events. To elevate your thoughts, seek out and surround yourself with positive influences and gradually focus more on substantial, uplifting conversations.

There are meaningful and purposeful words, and then there are meaningless and harmful ones. Reflect on the kind of words you hear throughout the day. Engaging in unnecessary gossip is a significant waste of time and energy, leading to unproductive use of our time. Such activities are a form of violent communication, wasting our precious time and life. Analyse how much time you spend on productive activities. Many people spend their precious time engaging in meaningless activities and thoughts: anarth dand or purposeless actions. This can include unnecessary talking, listening, and thinking. Many young people misuse their potential by engaging in such worthless activities. To make a positive change, reflect on the quality of your conversations and time use. Surround yourself with positive influences and focus on meaningful interactions, to lead a more productive and fulfilling life.

In the chapter Unnecessary Thinking, we explored Tandul matsya's obsession with Raghava matsya. The story witnessed how his unproductive thinking led to negative consequences despite his inaction. Despite its tiny size and inability to act, Tandul matsya's harmful and greedy thoughts led to its rebirth in the seventh hell. Raghava matsya also ended up in hell for his actions. This story powerfully highlights how even purposeless, idle or negative thinking can have severe karmic consequences.

The question here arises: how did a creature who never physically harmed or touched another being, and who couldn't possibly eat a fish, ends up in the seventh hell just because of its thoughts? This story emphasises the importance of our thoughts and the mental dispositions we cultivate. Even if our actions are harmless, harbouring harmful thoughts can have significant consequences. Harmless creatures can also accumulate negative karma, simply from their thoughts alone.

The internal processes of our body mimic our thoughts as if we are experiencing them in real life. A study demonstrated this by having an Olympic runner imagine a 400-metre race. He was connected to sensors. Despite no physical activity, his heart rate, blood pressure, and brain activity mirrored those of an athlete running the race. This experiment illustrates the powerful connection between our thoughts and our physical state, highlighting the significance of our thoughts and how they can manifest physically, impacting our overall well-being. It serves as a reminder to cultivate positive and meaningful thinking to lead a healthier and more fulfilling life.

Another example to illustrate this point: Suppose you are dreaming that your house is on fire. You see the fire spreading towards your bedroom, and it gets closer and closer until you feel, it will burn your bed. Suddenly, you wake up. How do you feel at that moment? Check your heart rate—it will likely be elevated. Although there was no real fire, your mind's reaction caused your body to respond, as if it were real. This phenomenon shows how powerful our thoughts are, and how they can elicit physical responses.

Among our actions, thoughts, and speech, we tend to make the most mistakes through our thoughts. Often, someone may seem virtuous to the world, yet they engage in violence, deceit and dishonesty. For example, when you travel, the ticket inspector does not always check the ticket, making it tempting to travel without a ticket. This illustrates how people with violent thoughts are prone to committing the most sins, followed by those who express violence through their words, and finally, through their actions.

Most of your life is spent on unnecessary listening, unnecessary thinking, and unnecessary activities, which lead to ruin. To achieve nonviolence in thought, communication, and life, one should cultivate these four key sentiments:

- Friendship: Love and friendship prevent us from criticising those we care about.
- Joy: Appreciating others qualities, reduces jealousy and competition.

- Compassion: Empathy and compassion stop us from thinking or speaking harmfully.
- Neutrality: Maintaining neutrality towards those who oppose us, eliminates animosity.

When these feelings are deeply ingrained, our thinking and communication will improve, and our lives will naturally become nonviolent. Acharya Umaswamiji taught these principles a thousand years ago, emphasising that internalising these sentiments will lead to positive thoughts, words, behaviours, and relationships.

To avoid the detrimental effects of violent thoughts, we must cultivate a nonviolent mindset. This begins with recognising and changing our thought processes. Our thoughts should be meaningful and purposeful, aiming to bring positivity and productivity into our lives. Only then can we transform our communication and behaviour, into something constructive and harmonious.

Actionables

- Analyse and see, how much time you spend with different individuals in twenty-four hours.
- Analyse how much time you have spent on constructive or productive activities.
- Can you recognise how often you become, like the Tandul matsya in real life?

Reminders:

- The violent thought process, that precedes violent communication is the most dangerous.
- According to the principle of karma, it does not matter whether we commit acts of violence in real life; what truly matters is our thoughts.
- Many young people misuse their potential by engaging in useless activities. Misusing talent is also a form of violent communication.
- To achieve nonviolence in thought, communication, and life, one should cultivate the four key sentiments: friendship, joy, compassion and neutrality.

SIX PRINCIPLES FOR GOOD PARENTING

THIS CHAPTER EXPLORES EFFECTIVE PARENTING, WHICH begins with careful observation and guidance of a child's activities. There are six key principles: hearing, seeing, eating, thinking, speaking, and doing. Parents can keep their children on the right path by monitoring these aspects. A child's future is not determined alone; parents, especially the mother play a crucial role in shaping it. So, what are you exposing your child to?

Let us recall an incident from the Mahabharata. Do you remember who Abhimanyu's parents were? They were Subhadra and Arjuna. One night, Arjuna was explaining something to Subhadra. He was teaching her how to enter a chakravyuh—a complex military formation—how to penetrate it, defeat the enemy, and emerge victorious. Subhadra listened attentively, but when Arjuna began explaining how to exit the chakravyuh, she fell asleep. This turned out to be a significant mistake. What was the consequence of this error? In the Mahabharata, Abhimanyu was killed. Had Subhadra not fallen asleep, this might have been avoided. This was because as a child, Abhimanyu was absorbing all of his father's conversations while he was still in his mother's womb. However, when Subhadra fell asleep, the connection to the outside world and to his father's teachings was lost. Similarly, many mothers today are adept at teaching their children how to enter the world—the worldly chakravyuh—but when it comes to guiding them on how to navigate their way out of life's complexities, they seem to fall asleep. Isn't that true? In that case, how can parents ensure this doesn't happen in their approach to parenting?

A child's journey in this world begins with hearing. The first skill they develop is the ability to listen. Following this, the child starts to see—when they are born and enter the world, their first instinct is to open their eyes and observe their surroundings. After this initial observation, the child cries and in response, they are fed milk, marking the beginning of their third activity—eating or drinking. As they continue to grow, their thought processes start to develop, leading to the fourth activity: thinking. With time, the child begins to speak, which is the fifth activity. Finally, the sixth activity is doing—taking action as they start to engage with the world around them.

A child's ability to learn and grasp new information is remarkably sharp. You might recall that when you were very young, it was easy to learn and memorise much more easily than you can do now. At that age, your learning capacity was at its peak. Children can absorb information quickly, often outpacing their parents. This is when they begin to learn what to think, see, hear, eat, speak, and do—forming the foundation of their development. Just as a building's strength relies on a stable foundation, a child's future depends on how solid this early foundation is. If it is weak, even a seemingly impressive structure will be unstable.

From an early age, if a child constantly hears demotivating words, it shapes their perception of themselves and their capabilities accordingly. As they grow up, consider the kind of language they are constantly being exposed to—from parents, relatives, society, friends, at the temple, outside, or at school. Are these words motivating or discouraging? What does your child listen to all day? Understand that the words they hear, will influence what they learn and eventually who they become.

Many parents unknowingly label their children with negative terms like 'fool' or say things like, 'You can't achieve anything in life,' 'You couldn't even manage this,' 'Your marks are so low,' 'Look at the neighbour's child—they got 99 per cent,' or 'Don't you have a brain?' Some children repeatedly hear phrases like, 'You don't know anything, you're a fool.' But how often do you hear a mother tell her child, 'You are very intelligent,' 'You have great potential,' 'You can achieve anything in life,' or 'Don't worry, you're doing great!' If you praise your child once, but call them a donkey, fool, or idiot several times, these negative labels get ingrained in their subconscious. They begin to doubt themselves and start believing, 'I don't know anything,' 'I'm not capable,' and 'Other kids are better than me.' It may start with the child, but who is truly responsible if a child starts believing that they're not good enough?

How do you respond when your child makes a mistake? If they get low marks in an exam, how do you handle it and help them move forward? If they drop a small glass, do you explain it to them constructively or destructively? Your approach in these moments can either build them up or tear them down.

Demotivating words are the worst form of violence. They represent a type of violent communication—words that deeply undermine a child's confidence. In the early stages of life, when a child's brain, body, and mindset are still developing, the words they hear shape their self-perception. If they are exposed to negative language during this crucial phase, they may begin to internalise those beliefs about themselves. If you want to see your child excel, it must start with positive, motivational, and kind words.

Another crucial aspect of learning for a child is through what they see with their eyes. A child's eyes work like a video camera, capturing and absorbing everything around them. You can tell them what to do, but they learn most effectively by observing. Just one glance can create a lasting image in their mind. For instance, if they see both parents on their phones all day, they will naturally imitate that behaviour. Children watch everything you do, including how much time you spend on your phone. Instead of connecting with them during quality time, if you hand them a mobile device, they may become addicted to it—and later, you might find yourself complaining that they do not listen or that they are too attached to their screens. When they needed a mother's love, they were given cartoons on a mobile instead. As they grow up, they may start to mirror the behaviours they observed from those cartoons. During a critical phase when they should have received love, affection, and kind words from their mother, what were they actually exposed to? What did their eyes mostly see and absorb during this formative period?

Another important aspect of a child's development is their eating habits. Have you wondered, what is it that you are feeding them? Often, due to a lack of time, parents resort to giving their children junk food or packaged food. Why is it called junk food? Because it has low nutritional value—essentially zero nutrition. Packaged foods generally offer negligible, or very low nutritional benefits. When you give your child junk food or fast food, you're offering them something quick and easy to prepare, like two-minute noodles. However, these foods are typically made from refined flour, which has little to no nutritional value and can even stick to their intestines. In the long run, these choices can harm their health and general development.

The fourth key activity is teaching your child how to think. Remember, a child's learning begins even before birth—well before pregnancy. Giving birth to a child is akin to a farmer planting a seed and nurturing it into a fully grown tree. The process does not start at the last moment; the farmer prepares for it, months in advance. Similarly, before becoming parents, a husband and wife need to cultivate their thoughts and mindset well in advance, ideally six months before conception. The mindset of the parents should align with the virtues of the Tirthankaras—the twenty-four revered and enlightened spiritual teachers in Jainism, who guide the path to salvation—setting the foundation for the birth of a capable and virtuous child.

The fifth and most important aspect is teaching your child what to speak and how to speak. Every mother and father should carefully observe what their child says and work to purify their speech. Establish a rule that when the child wakes up in the morning, they should begin the day by saying something positive—a good name, a mantra, or the name of a respected person or deity. Just as you use a toothbrush to clean your teeth, you should use good words to cleanse the tongue from all negativity at the start of the day.

The first step of the day is crucial. If that step is in the right direction, the rest of the day is likely to follow suit. Conversely, if the first step is wrong, it can set a negative tone for the rest of the day. Therefore, it is vital to ensure that the first words your child speaks are positive and meaningful. Teach them the importance of starting the day with good speech, especially during their early years, as this will significantly influence their future.

The final key activity is determining what you engage your child in. How many mothers aspire for their child to be religious, cultured, and virtuous like a Tirthankara? If you wish to see your son become a Tirthankara or a great person, remember that you must first embody the qualities of a Tirthankara's mother. If you want your child to achieve greatness, you must first elevate yourself from within, not just in outward appearance. This is essential to understand.

One of the greatest gifts a mother can offer her child is the early cultivation of right conduct through small, consistent actions. Taking them to the temple, encouraging दान (daan) or charitable giving, and instilling awareness of ahimsa (nonviolence)—even toward the smallest beings like ants or insects—help develop empathy, compassion, and a sense of responsibility. These practices, when made part of daily life, shape the child's moral compass and spiritual foundation. They become not just habits, but samskaras—deep impressions that influence not only this life but future lifetimes, ensuring that something essential and noble is never missing from their character.

Now, consider the activities you have them do, throughout the day. You ensure they complete their school homework, assignments, and projects, but have you ever taught them to visit the temple, put a coin in the donation box, or show respect by touching the feet of a guru? These actions are just as crucial for their development.

Becoming a parent is easy, but becoming a good parent requires significant sacrifice and preparation. Ideally, the journey to parenthood should begin six months in advance, with parents cultivating a clear and pure mindset, much like the parents of Tirthankaras, even if their child may not become one. This preparation demands sacrifices, the relinquishing of comforts, and an improvement in one's thoughts, speech, eating habits, thinking patterns, and actions. To give birth to a child of high moral and intellectual standing, parents must focus on thinking well, seeing well, speaking well, listening well, eating well, and acting well—in those crucial six months before conception.

Unfortunately, today's parents often do not prepare, and everything becomes accidental—leading to uncertain outcomes regarding the child's future. If none of the six key activities are done properly—if the child is not exposed to good words, healthy food, and positive examples—the results may not align with the parents hopes. How many parents truly teach their children to see well, speak well, listen well, eat well, act well, and think well? These practices are essential not just for the child, but for the parents themselves. When we embody these values, the children around us will naturally follow our example.

Actionables

How do you effectively inculcate these six fundamental activities—hearing, seeing, eating, thinking, speaking, and doing—in your child?

Activity	How do you nurture each one?
Hearing	
Seeing	
Eating	
Thinking	
Speaking	
Doing	

Reminders:

- Parents can keep their children on the right path by monitoring these six aspects: hearing, seeing, eating, thinking, speaking, and doing.
- A child's future is not determined alone; parents, especially the mother, play a crucial role.
- A child's eyes work like a video camera, capturing and absorbing everything around them.
- When the child wakes up in the morning, they should begin the day by saying something positive—a good name, a mantra, or the name of a respected person or deity.
- Demotivating words are the worst form of violence.

MATHEMATICS OF FAMILY: 1+1= -11 OR 1+1=11

THE WAY WE SEE AND INTERPRET THE WORLD AROUND us has a big impact on how we shape our lives and stay organised. While we cannot always control our surroundings, we can control how we respond to them. The same situation can be experienced as either positive or negative—depending on our perspective. The key to improving our lives, lies in focusing on our responses rather than external conditions. Self-reflection and a positive outlook towards life are crucial for creating happiness.

Blaming others for our failures and attributing successes solely to ourselves, often leads to missed opportunities for self-growth. To lead a fulfilling life, we should acknowledge the contributions others make towards our achievements, and approach both success and failure with humility. By adopting this perspective, we cultivate progress, joy, and positivity, even when outcomes do not align with our expectations.

To improve our lives, we should adopt an inward-looking perspective rather than blaming external factors. Instead of attributing problems to others—like family, colleagues, or friends, we should focus on our own responses and attitudes. An inward-looking perspective helps us to navigate challenges effectively, while an outward-looking one often leads to distress.

Most people have complaints about how others treat them or fail to understand them. If someone or something has not changed over a long period, it indicates that our approach may need re-evaluation. Both sides may hold their own views but if the outcomes are consistently negative, it suggests that neither perspective may be entirely correct. In relationships, compatibility can enhance positivity, while its absence can lead to negative results. With compatibility, one plus one can feel like more than two—like eleven—whereas without it, one plus one might even result in negative outcomes. Complaints and blaming each other often point to faults in our own approach. When perspectives remain unchanged over decades, it reflects a static situation where neither side has evolved.

Just as opposite poles of a magnet attract, life's dynamics should ideally create attraction rather than conflict. Constant dissatisfaction often signals that we are focusing outwards, rather than examining our own role in the situation.

If we want to live happily and achieve something in life, we must first learn to change our perspective. Regardless of how things are or how they appear, once our perspective changes, much will begin to change, and everything will start to shift.

Many people excel at managing external responsibilities—such as financial management or running organisations—but struggle with managing their own lives. Life management is crucial, yet even those who manage others well often fail to create a fulfilling personal life. It's worth considering whether managing your personal life is more important than your external roles. Difficulties in managing family life, household organisation, or relationships often stem from a lack of bonding and harmony. Despite high education and career success, people may fail to see what's truly important or experience genuine happiness.

We want other people to deliver what they cannot. We push them beyond their capabilities. A mango cannot turn into a tamarind, and a tamarind cannot turn into a mango. Things will remain as they are, so why do you expect to see a mango in a tamarind? Where feelings and emotions align, where both people understand each other's nature and expectations.

Let me tell you a small, real and quite interesting story. A man from a very small village visits a metro city. He had heard a lot about the city and decided to explore it. With great enthusiasm, he roams around the city, taking in all the sights. One day, he decided to visit a very large zoo, with many animals. It was his first time seeing so many creatures in one place; a fierce lion in a cage, a bear in another area, deer, monkeys, peacocks, and all sorts of animals.

After wandering around for hours, by noon, he sat down, holding his head in his hands. The zoo manager noticed him and came over to inquire if something was wrong. The man replied, 'I've explored your entire zoo and have seen all these animals, but I'm not able to understand something.'

The manager, curious, asked what he did not understand. The man explained, 'When I see these monkeys jumping around so much, a question arises in my mind. Is there any way you could make these monkeys sit quietly, like that turtle over there? Look at how calmly it is sitting. And not just that, they eat a little and then throw the rest around, creating such a mess. Isn't there some way to manage them better so they do not cause so much trouble? They climb trees, which is fine, but at least they should not waste the fruits they pick. They take a bite and then toss the rest away, wasting so much. All your hard work is going to waste because of them.'

Then, pointing to the birds flying freely in the sky, he continued, 'Look at these birds, flying in the open sky without any restrictions. They have no boundaries. And these fish swimming in the pond, can't you do something so that these fish, with their fins, can fly in the sky like the birds? For the first time, I have seen golden crows. In my village, all the crows are black, but these golden crows, even with their beautiful bodies, only make the same caw-caw sound. They look so beautiful, but whenever they open their beaks, all that comes out is caw-caw-caw. In my village, we have cuckoos that sing so sweetly. Why don't these golden crows produce a melodious sound like the cuckoo? Can't you do something about it?'

Now, the zoo manager was frustrated after a visitor requested impossible changes: crows sounding like cuckoos, fish flying, and monkeys sitting quietly like turtles. Despite all efforts, a crow will always caw, and a monkey will jump around—it is their nature. Similarly, people cannot change their fundamental nature.

If you want to live happily, accept others as they are. Just as animals have distinct traits, so do your family members. You cannot change your parents, spouse, or children to meet your expectations. Instead, create a framework—to understand and adapt to their inherent nature. Recognise that each person has their own qualities—some may be like a monkey, a golden crow, a turtle, a flying bird, or a swimming fish. Embracing this perspective, will help you avoid expecting them to be something they are not.

To truly transform your life, shift from an outward perspective to an inward one. Instead of focusing on external circumstances, reflect on your own essence. Expecting a crow to sing like a cuckoo or a monkey to act like a turtle is unrealistic. If you cannot change yourself to fit a desired role, why expect others to do so? By adapting to others nature and meeting their needs, you may find that they will adjust to you in return. Transformations in life, family, and relationships often begin with how we change ourselves, leading to greater joy and happiness.

Understand this: either let go of your expectations from others, or if you desire something from them, first fulfil their needs. To see change in your life, start by changing yourself. Trying to mould others without understanding the process is futile. To uplift someone, you must first lower yourself to their level. It is a give-and-take dynamic—first, you give, and then you receive.

If you want to achieve something, be prepared to sacrifice, overcome fears, or compromise. Rigid expectations from others, without self-change will only lead to frustration. Effective management begins at home and requires a balanced approach. Without this understanding, your family may become just a place to stay, and true happiness will remain out of reach. In family dynamics, 1+1 can either equals 11 or -11: depending on your perspective. Embrace introspection and adopt an inward-focused mindset for a harmonious life.

Actionables

1.	Embrace others as they are	Develop a framework to understand and adapt to the diverse qualities and behaviours of your family members.
2.	Shift from an outward to an inward perspective	Reflect on your own behaviours and mindset rather than focusing on external circumstances.
3.	Adopt an introspective and balanced approach	Engage in introspection to understand your own role in family dynamics and personal happiness.

Reminders:

- Transformations in life, family, and relationships often begin with how we change ourselves, leading to greater joy and happiness.
- To see change in your life, start by changing yourself. In family dynamics, 1 + 1 can equal 11 or -11, depending on your perspective.
- You cannot change your parents, spouse, or children to meet your expectations. Instead, create a framework to understand and adapt to their inherent nature.

PART 5

PERSONAL GROWTH AND RESILIENCE

EASY WAYS TO GET RELIEF FROM ANXIETY

EVERYONE DESIRES HAPPINESS, BUT IT OFTEN SEEMS scarce while sorrow is abundant. This suggests errors in our approach. If after years of effort, the goal seems farther away, we must be on the wrong path. Movement alone is not enough; it must be in the right direction. Slow progress in the right direction is better than rushing the wrong way. Reflect on whether your life's direction is correct. Recognising and facing the right path is an achievement, even if you have not started walking yet.

Life is a continuous journey, constantly in motion. Many people drift aimlessly without purpose, but unique results require a unique path. Meeting influential figures is less important, than the changes they inspire within us. What is your goal? We desire happiness, but how do we achieve it? Worry arises when we think about unachieved desires. Can we prevent these desires from emerging? Worry often stems from concerns about the future, or dwelling on the past such as, job security, relationships, or health. This fear of uncertainty outcomes triggers anxiety.

Everyone desires a better future, and while the past cannot be changed, our present actions shape what is to come. Focusing on the present is crucial for a good future. Dwelling on the past and stressing over it, yields no positive results. Life should be about forward progression, not backward regression. Learning from our past mistakes is valuable, as these lessons guide us on the right path. Many people get stuck in regret, thinking about missed opportunities and what ifs. For example, not investing when property rates are low, or missing stock market opportunities. Instead of getting trapped in regret, we should learn from the past and focus on shaping a better future. This proactive approach is the right attitude toward life.

Acharya Kundkund Maharaj emphasises understanding attachment and detachment through everyday examples. Recognising the impermanence of objects helps cultivate detachment, and avoid emotional entanglement. For instance, acknowledging the temporary nature of a hotel room or the transient beauty of a rose prevents attachment. Similarly, accepting inevitable separation on a train journey diminishes sadness. The key is to see the impermanence of things, preventing desire and attachment.

Living with this mindset means—enjoying life without getting entangled in worldly desires. Like the tongue, which tastes food but remains unaffected, one can experience life fully while staying detached. Even if complete desirelessness is unattainable, understanding this perspective reduces life's problems and prevents getting stuck.

A wise person anticipates and prepares for future events, much like a driver adjusting speed when seeing a brake light. By recognising the true essence of experiences and anticipating future changes, one can live comfortably and avoid unnecessary worries. The difference between the knowledgeable and the ignorant, lies in seeing the complete picture and understanding—both visible and invisible aspects of life.

In summary, we cannot fully transcend desires, but by recognising their impermanent nature and practicing detachment, we can live with fewer worries and greater ease. This understanding helps us navigate life's journey more wisely and safely. Living in this way, one sees the world realistically, recognising separation at the time of union and death at birth. This recognition prevents new desires from arising, allowing one to live beyond worldly desires, while still engaging in life's activities.

Relief, joy, and happiness in life come when one anticipates future events, and prepares for them. This may seem tough, but the solution lies, in not creating unrealistic expectations for the future. By recognising the potential for separation or loss in every situation, one can manage expectations and avoid disappointment.

For example, if you know a customer might cheat you or a property deal could go wrong, you would avoid these situations to protect yourself. Similarly, you should apply this foresight, to your mind and emotions. Just as a cat mistakenly believes it is safe—when it closes its eyes while drinking milk, we often ignore potential future issues, that are leading to unnecessary problems. Always being prepared for the worst, can help you live a tension-free life. By visualising possible outcomes and preparing for them, you can manage your expectations and reduce anxiety. This proactive approach, allows you to handle life's uncertainties with greater ease and resilience.

Actionables

- What is your goal? Is finding happiness your goal in life?
- Which paths have you tried to achieve happiness in?
- Make a list of things that trigger your anxiety.

Reminders:

- Slow progress in the right direction, is better than rushing the wrong way.
- Always being prepared for the worst, can help you live a tension-free life
- Relief, joy, and happiness in life come, when one anticipates future events and prepares for them.
- We cannot fully transcend desires, but by recognising their impermanent nature and practicing detachment, we can live with fewer worries and greater ease.

WAYS TO ATTAIN FREEDOM FROM FEAR

We all strive for happiness and progress, but fear often holds us back. Why do we feel afraid when we are taking steps forward in any task? Many people plan but hesitate when it is time to act, fearing failure and its consequences. This fear can create mental barriers for many. What situations trigger fear within us? In what areas do we feel it? When, where, and from whom does it arise? Understanding these questions is crucial. Until we don't grasp the why, we cannot overcome it effectively. What is the root cause of fear? We are searching for it. Understanding and overcoming this fear is key to achieving our goals, but until now we are only wandering in the periphery and haven't reached the centre yet.

Fear manifests in two scenarios: when we desire something and fear not attaining it, or when we possess something and fear losing it. Both cases often stem from attachment and intense desires. Fear often revolves around losing respect, dignity, and witnessing the suffering of loved ones. There is also the fear of tarnishing one's family name, and the worry of enemies when in power. Reputation is a significant concern for many. Interestingly, having wealth does not guarantee a peace of mind. Those with little wealth may sleep well—due to having less to lose, while those with vast empires fear losing everything. For someone with very little, the fear may stem from the uncertainty of meeting basic needs, or losing what little they have.

Can we truly overcome fear in real life? Ideally yes, by transcending our desires. The main reason behind fear is often our excessive desire for acquisition, which spans various aspects of life. These desires range—from necessities, to aspirations for fame and more. Rising above one's desire is the key to becoming fearless.

To overcome fear, we must identify its root cause. Let us illustrate this with an example. Imagine, a seed planted in soil that suddenly stops growing. A person frets over this and begins watering the roots, believing that it is the solution. Yet, growth does not occur. Seeking advice, they discover insects infesting the roots. Removing these pests is crucial for water absorption. Similarly, to conquer fear, we must identify and address the underlying issues. It is like watering the roots; we need to eliminate the obstacles hindering our self-growth. Though we may know what to do—like watering the roots, sometimes the hidden obstacles—like the insects, evade our sight.

We must understand who or what we fear, why, and to what extent. While a complete solution may not always be feasible, learning to manage fear can be invaluable in life, offering significant benefits even amidst challenges. People often die many times before their actual death due to the fear of dying. While physically alive, mentally they may already be dead. Fear can lead to multiple deaths throughout life. Covid-19 exemplified how fear itself can be fatal, with many succumbing not to the virus but to the anxiety surrounding it. Despite the odds, a strong belief in oneself can overcome seemingly impossible challenges.

In times of crisis—whether personal, societal, or global—fear often spreads as swiftly as the crisis itself, sometimes even faster. Mass hysteria can take root, compounding the challenges at hand. While managing the physical aspects of a disease or disaster is crucial, equal attention must be paid to the psychological toll it takes on individuals and communities. Resilience training becomes essential—not only as a long-term mental health strategy but as an immediate tool to manage fear constructively. Just as we develop medical treatments to fight illness, we must also cultivate emotional preparedness as a form of psychological first aid. Compassionate communication plays a vital role here, enabling us to acknowledge fear without amplifying it, while nurturing trust, emotional connection, and a sense of safety.

To live fearlessly, cultivating self-confidence is crucial. There is an interesting story highlighting the power of belief and confidence. In this scenario a small kingdom faced a formidable opponent, and when confronted with the reality of an impending battle, the commander suggested turning to divine intervention through a coin toss. Interestingly, the coin came up heads repeatedly, leading the army to believe that God was on their side, filling them with courage and determination. Despite being outnumbered and facing a superior opponent, the small army emerged victorious in battle, while the larger enemy forces suffered defeat. However, when the truth about the coin having heads on both sides was revealed, it was not divine intervention that won the battle, but rather the confidence instilled in the soldiers by the belief that they had divine support.

This story underscores the importance of self-confidence, and belief in oneself. While external factors may seem daunting, having faith in one's abilities can lead to success, even in the face of adversity. It also serves as a reminder—to not succumb to defeat before even trying, as victory often lies in perseverance and self-belief.

Understand why your confidence wavers initially. Instead of focusing on those struggling, observe those who are brimming with self-assurance. Shift your perspective. Are you fixated on problems or possibilities? Like attracts like; the universe mirrors your energy—what you radiate in thought, feeling, or intention is reflected back to you. So, it's not just what we perceive, but how we perceive it. The key is not what we think but how we think. Likewise, it's not merely what we say or do, but how we say and do it. Shift your focus from what to how. It is not about changing the world or others; it is about changing how we interact with them.

Let us read a story about a donkey. In a village, there was a washerman who used to load clothes on his donkey and take them away. One day, after an hour, the donkey fell into a deep well. It had a little water, along with stones and mud at the bottom. So, the donkey fell into the well but didn't die. While searching for his donkey, the washerman reached the well and peered inside. He saw the donkey there and thought: 'The well is so deep, it will cost so much to get him out. Why should I spend so much? Let me forget about getting him out. Just like we bury him after he dies, let me put some mud on him, and he will bury himself.'

On the other hand, the donkey was deep in the well thinking that his master is so kind for throwing mud to save him. As the dirt fell on him, the donkey rose as the well slowly began filling up. While the master was busy burying the donkey thinking of only escaping the saving cost; the donkey thought his master to be so compassionate—thinking he was helping him rise by throwing dirt into the well.

Whether something is a stumbling block or a stepping stone depends on how you use it. What you are receiving in your life can be either a stumbling block or a stepping stone. You must decide. You can take it as a barrier in your life, where someone is throwing stones at you. Or you can take those stumbling blocks and stones, pile them up, and make a ladder to climb up. It is up to you. What is crucial is how you want to perceive and deal with life's challenges, and not how it exists.

Instead of comparing ourselves to others, we should focus on those who thrive despite difficulties. Shift your mindset from dwelling on failure to embracing lessons learned and skills gained. Each person's journey is unique, so focus on learning from those who have overcome obstacles and achieved success. Change your perspective and approach to grow and overcome challenges.

Indeed, the simplest way to deal with fear is to confront it directly. We can overcome the fear of trying by trying. We must be willing to act, even if it means facing discomfort or setbacks. Those who confront their fears directly, seldom encounter insurmountable obstacles in life. Consider a child learning to ride a bicycle. They may stumble and get hurt, but if they focus solely on the falls, they will develop a fear of riding altogether. Similarly, to conquer the fear of water, one must dive in.

Accepting that setbacks are part of the process is a crucial way to attain gradual freedom from our fears. Facing fear with inner confidence is essential for one's progress. Doctors suggest facing what scares us; even poison can become medicine with gradual exposure. Just as a child gains confidence in walking—by taking small steps and falling, we too can build confidence through gradual attempts. Overcoming fear requires facing it fearlessly.

Actionables

Note down:

- What fears do you have?
- How much fear do you feel?
- Whose failure is making us scared?
- Why is fear arising?
    - Is it because of someone?
    - Is it because of the surroundings?
    - Is it because we doubt our capabilities?
    - Is it because we have not tried yet?

Reminders:

- The only way to overcome fear, is to face what scares you.
- One should not succumb to defeat before even trying, as victory often lies in perseverance and self-belief.
- Learn to observe those who are filled with self-confidence, rather than those who are full of doubts.
- We often forget that everyone's journey is unique. We need to stop comparing ourselves to those who have failed; and start looking at those who have overcome obstacles, and achieved success despite challenges.

LIFE BEGINS AT THE END OF THE COMFORT ZONE

LIFE BEGINS WHEN WE STEP OUT OF OUR COMFORT zone, yet everyone prefers to stay within their own comfort zone. They enjoy it and believe that stepping out will only bring problems and hardships. However, those who embrace and overcome life's adversities, often experience profound and unique transformations in their lives. People often fear the difficulties and challenges that life may bring, wishing they would not face any tough periods. Aren't we all afraid? How many people are truly ready to face hardships? There is a key difference between being prepared to face challenges, and hoping they never arise. Some individuals accept challenges—as an inevitable and necessary part of life, understanding that they are crucial for growth.

Essentially, there are three types of people in this context.

The first type of individual hopes for a life free of obstacles, desiring a smooth and trouble-free existence, whether the challenges are physical or mental. About 95 per cent of people fall into this category, believing their future should be bright and untroubled.

The second type is more practical. While they also wish for a positive future, they prepare themselves to face challenges when they arise. They adopt a mindset of tackling difficulties head-on, making plans to address adversities as they come. This type is relatively rare.

The third type shares the goal of a good future but takes it further. Not only are they internally prepared for challenges, but they actively seek out and embrace difficulties. They step forward to confront obstacles, which may seem extreme to some. This category is exceptional; such individuals are crucial for refining, purifying, and elevating life. Ideally, we should not wait for adversities to come our way, but should proactively embrace and prepare for them. Those in the third category are extraordinary, and it is by adopting such a mindset that life reaches its highest potential. Hence, it is said that life truly begins at the end of your comfort zone.

A top-class cricket player reaches the top position not just by reading about cricket, but through extensive practice. They spend six hours daily in net practice, sweating it out without any guarantee of selection. Even after being selected for the team, they keep practicing for hours, to ensure their performance remains at its peak. This persistence is necessary—because without continually striving and adapting, one cannot sustain their position at the top. It is through enduring and overcoming challenges, that true excellence is achieved.

Here is an interesting story: A young child was playing at home when he noticed a bird's egg in the corner. The egg had fallen and cracked open, revealing a tiny chick inside. The chick struggled to get out because the egg had broken prematurely. It tried to climb out but kept slipping back inside, due to the sticky material inside the egg. Seeing the chick's struggle, the child decided to help. He took a pencil and gently supported the chick by inserting the pencil into the egg. This helped the chick get a better grip, and eventually climb out successfully. The child felt a great sense of accomplishment, having helped the little chick escape from its predicament. The child was thrilled to have made a significant difference, by assisting the chick in its time of need.

The child excitedly ran to tell his father, 'Daddy, I did something great today! I helped a little chick get out of its egg by supporting it with a pencil.' When the father heard this, he responded differently than expected. Instead of praising the child, he asked, 'What did you do?' The child was surprised, thinking his father would be pleased and proud but instead, his father's reaction was questioning and concerned. When they went to see the chick, it had managed to come out of the egg and was moving very slowly on the floor. Eventually, it would not be able to survive, because it had not developed the strength it needed to live on its own. The father told the child, 'You didn't do the right thing.' The child asked, 'What was wrong with what I did?' The father explained, 'The mistake was in giving support. Providing support in this situation was a big mistake.' The father's point was that while the child's intention was good, his well-meaning help had ultimately hindered the chick's chances of survival.

The child was confused. 'How can giving support be wrong?' he asked. The father responded, 'Yes, it can be wrong. The support should have been given at the right time, but what you did was interfere with the chick's natural struggle. The struggle to get out of the egg, and the sticky material inside were necessary for strengthening the chick's wings and legs. Each time the chick fell, it was becoming stronger and developing the force needed to survive. If you had allowed the chick to fight its way out on its own, its body would have become strong enough to thrive in the world. Not only would it have survived, but it would have been capable of flying high in the sky. The struggle was not a curse but a blessing. By giving support too early, you prevented the chick from developing its full potential. Your well-intentioned help was a hindrance.'

The father emphasised that the struggle and the effort required for the chick to get out of the egg were crucial for its growth and survival. The child's emotional decision to help had inadvertently taken away the chick's opportunity to develop the strength it needed.

So, the question was: Did the child do the right thing? The answer was clear: No, the child's action, though well-meaning, had not been correct. The struggle was a blessing and not a curse, as it was essential for the chick's growth.

Understand this: Whenever we face difficulties or adversities in our lives, it is considered to be a golden period. If we can learn and gain wisdom during these times, we realise that these challenges are not curses, but opportunities for our growth. Difficulties are not merely obstacles; they are blessings in disguise that help us develop and shine. In life, some people crumble under such circumstances, while only a few rise and excel. Are you among those who falter or those who rise to the occasion? Most people prefer not to face difficulties and resist stepping out of their comfort zones. Do you want to move beyond your comfort zone? Whenever you are told to step out of your comfort zone, do you hesitate? The more you stay within your comfort zone, the weaker you become—both physically and mentally. It is true.

Major health issues like heart disease, diabetes, high cholesterol, and mental health conditions such as—anxiety, stress, and depression are common. In contrast, construction workers and labourers who toil under the sun from early morning to late at night every day, with minimal food, often live without air conditioning, proper housing, or vehicles. Their diet typically consists of just dry bread, chili, jaggery, and onions, yet they remain fit and healthy. On the other hand, many people who live in air-conditioned environments—air-conditioned bedrooms, offices, and cars—often suffer from various health problems such as diabetes, high blood pressure, high cholesterol, arthritis, spondylosis, cervical issues, migraines, and high-stress levels. Despite having access to high-quality food rich in proteins, minerals, vitamins, and carbohydrates, and enjoying top-notch facilities at home and at work, they still face these health issues.

You enjoy all the comforts and amenities, and yet you are living a very comfortable life. These merits or luxuries known as पुण्य *(punya)* are the result of good deeds from your past, the benefits of which you are reaping in the present. However, despite this comfort, the results—whether physical, mental, or spiritual—are not always positive. Even with the best diet and facilities, the question remains: Why are these health issues occurring? The answer lies not just in material comforts, but also in how we handle and understand our well-being. People who step out of their comfort zones, end up strengthening their lives in every way. They become strong and resilient, never remaining weak.

Our lives are refined through difficulties and adversities. These challenges are not curses but blessings. However, the mindset of most people is to avoid such challenges. You have a mindset that adversities should not come your way. Instead, you should develop the mindset that adversities are necessary. Otherwise, you will end up like the chick that died; you will die inside, you will break down, and your stress levels will rise dramatically. Many people are not truly living; they are merely existing, suffering in their daily lives. They live in name only, but their lives lack vitality.

Understand this well. Prepare yourself mentally. Whenever life does not go as planned, and you face adversities—whether physical, financial, or familial—know that these challenges are not meant to bring you down or scare you. Instead, they are meant to strengthen you. Just as gold refines and purifies through intense heat in a furnace, adversities refine and purify us, removing impurities and distortions.

Adversities are powerful tools for our growth. One should practice facing and dealing with adversities directly.

It is about preparing oneself in such a way that one might choose to eat less, live without air conditioning, or use public transportation instead of driving a car—embodying a sense of simplicity and restraint. Experiencing these things helps broaden one's perspective, and strengthens both physical and mental resilience.

Facing adversity directly and experiencing it firsthand, makes a person stronger and more resilient. Just as saints willingly face hardships to purify themselves and their actions, so too does experiencing discomfort—as it contributes to one's personal growth and resilience. Those who stay connected with nature and embrace simplicity become stronger, while those who constantly seek comfort and convenience tend to become weaker, both physically and mentally.

To elevate your mindset and strengthen yourself, always remember this principle: Life begins at the end of your comfort zone. When faced with adversity—do not panic, break down, or fear. Instead, view it as an opportunity for growth, not as a setback. Embrace these challenges as they will refine you, and elevate your life. By accepting and welcoming these experiences, you will become stronger inside and out. If you retreat from fear, you will only become more fearful and weaker.

Understand that everything you receive in life, including adverse situations, is a result of your actions. Do not let negativity consume you. Have dreams and goals, but also prepare yourself to be strong. This preparation will make your life much more fulfilling, and will help you shine brightly in the world.

Actionables

By taking the following actions, you can strengthen your physical and mental resilience. After each experience, reflect on how it felt and document your thoughts and observations.

1.	Reduce comforts	Turn off the air conditioning and live without it for a day, or a set period to experience the effects of not having this comfort.
2.	Use public transportation	Commit to using public transportation, instead of driving for a day or a set number of trips.
3.	Simplify your meals	Plan and prepare a meal using only basic ingredients, like what someone in poverty might have access to. Choose to eat a smaller portion or skip a meal to understand the experience of limited food availability.

Reminders:

- The more you stay within your comfort zone, the weaker you become—both physically and mentally. It is true.
- Adversities are powerful tools for our growth. If you start developing the right attitude towards these challenges, your mental strength will rise significantly.
- To elevate your mindset and strengthen yourself, always remember this principle: Life begins at the end of your comfort zone.

PART 6

CULTIVATING GRATITUDE AND REFLECTION

GRATITUDE IS THE KEY TO HAPPINESS AND PEACE

Many people in our lives may possess qualities that are difficult to appreciate, and we often focus more on their flaws rather than their positive attributes. Even if someone has 99 per cent good qualities, our ego directs our attention to the 1 per cent flaw. Everyone acknowledges that we should adopt an attitude—of recognising and accepting positive traits in others. Despite knowing this, we often struggle to see the good in those around us. Why do we focus on flaws more, and how can we shift our perspective to see the good instead? This habit of flaw-finding spans across all kinds of relationships, whether with younger individuals, elders, or even those who have helped us. The key is to train our perspective to notice and appreciate strengths rather than weaknesses. But how do we begin cultivating this more positive outlook?

This chapter explores the transformative power of gratitude. When we develop a sense of gratitude; the world around us becomes more pleasant, and even people we may not get along with, start to seem more agreeable and beneficial. This change in our mindsets will help us become the kind of person we aspire to be and achieve our desires.

Many people look back on moments of anger or arrogance with regret, thinking, 'I shouldn't have acted that way.' Why do we lose control in those moments? What can we do to prevent this? The answer lies in filling ourselves with gratitude. Gratitude not only calms our impulses but also supports our personal growth. By recognising and appreciating the support we receive, we can develop ourselves and become better individuals. Yet we often neglect to thank those who help us directly, and forget their contributions. We often tend to overlook the important people and things in our lives, focusing instead on those who do not impact us directly.

Start by remembering those who have made a difference in your life. Start with your parents. Above all, the greatest gratitude is reserved for those who gave us life and have supported us unconditionally. What feeling should we have towards them? Gratitude, love, and reverence—these are the pillars that uphold the very foundation of our existence.

Begin by acknowledging the immense sacrifice and nurturing provided by our mothers. This awareness can lead to a profound sense of gratitude, that transforms both our nature and relationships. The person who endures the most in life is often the mother. Have you had moments where you deeply reflected on this? To truly change ourselves and align our nature with our aspirations, we should start by feeling grateful towards our mother. In Indian culture, touching our parents' feet is a symbolic gesture that instils deep reverence and humility. Yet, many go through life without acknowledging their mother's importance. Following the mother, the role of the father is also crucial. Expressing heartfelt gratitude—not just through words but through meaningful actions, is essential towards those who have given us everything.

This spirit of gratitude extends beyond our parents. In Indian culture, even the basic elements like water, fire, air, and earth are respected as deities to cultivate gratitude for their essential roles in our existence. Have you ever felt thankful for the air you breathe? Without it, survival is impossible. This continuous gratitude leads to an internal transformation. We start treating the environment—and one another—with greater respect and care, and by recognising their vital contributions, we develop a positive connection with the world around us.

Let us consider the story of a German scholar who came to India to meet a renowned guru, highlighting a lesson in humility and gratitude. Instead of diving into meditation techniques, the guru asked him to apologise for slamming the door upon entering the room. Initially surprised, the scholar soon understood the deeper meaning: one must humble oneself and rectify their behaviour towards their surroundings to progress spiritually. Just as we must handle paper properly to write effectively, we must respect our environment and the elements that sustain us. This practice of sincere apology and acknowledgement—nurtures genuine gratitude and understanding, underscoring the importance of respecting our surroundings and elements.

This perspective cultivates deeper understanding and sensitivity, leading to more thoughtful behaviour and purer intentions.

The story highlights the importance of being aware and grateful towards every living being and natural element. Saints often teach us to seek forgiveness from all beings—whether living or non-living, to respect our surroundings and the objects that play significant roles in our lives.

We can observe similar expressions of gratitude in everyday life. In various sports, athletes often touch the ball to their forehead before kicking or throwing it, whether in football, cricket, or other sports. This gesture of respect reflects gratitude and acknowledgement, for what the sport gives them. Similarly, shopkeepers touch and pray to the shutter before opening their shop, recognising its crucial role in their livelihood. These acts are deeply emotional; signifying that without these sources of sustenance, people would have nothing. This is not merely about emotion or tradition; it is about developing our souls and elevating ourselves to the plane of humility.

Japanese culture offers a similar example. Before meals, people in Japan say *Itadakimasu*—a phrase expressing gratitude not just to the cook, but to all who made the meal possible, including nature itself. In martial arts, bowing to the dojo, teacher, and opponent reflects the same spirit. Such gestures show that gratitude transcends geography; it is a universal act of grounding ourselves in humility and connection.

The greatest characteristic of truly great people throughout history is—that they always remain filled with gratitude. They behave very well with every person and every object in every situation, because they have seen softness in it, whether in that object or in that person. So, where do we start cultivating this perspective? The answer lies in our everyday life, in our surroundings, and appreciating what we are getting. We can develop this attitude of thankfulness by acknowledging what we have received in life, the favours an object done for us, and the kindness we have received from others.

When this mindset of appreciation begins to take root within us, ego naturally dissolves. Anger no longer arises as easily, because we start to understand situations and people with more clarity and compassion. Our temperament begins to shift—marked not by irritation or entitlement, but by deep gratitude. When this inner transformation starts, even in small ways—toward a few people or a few objects—we begin to change. And as our perspective shifts, we no longer look for perfection in others. We begin to respect ourselves, and in doing so, we start to see only the goodness in those around us.

When one has a sense of gratitude, they make significant progress internally. Look at all the great people, whether leaders, politicians, saints, or entrepreneurs; a common trait is their deep sense of gratitude. They are not swayed or defeated by external criticism or praise because they operate from a place of humility and purpose. On the other hand, when we act without gratitude, our actions become self-serving. Without gratitude, even good deeds lose depth and meaning.

Start each day by reflecting on who has contributed to your life and begin with gratitude. Recall everyone who has given you something in life, from parents to teachers, friends, society, and spiritual guides. Remember their contributions, and maintain an attitude of gratitude. Life gradually transforms through this practice.

Gratitude is not just a polite gesture; it is a complete shift in our inner nature. It teaches us to bow down in appreciation, to acknowledge the value of even the smallest blessings. Saying thank you with sincerity has the power to soften our hearts and bring beauty into our lives. It helps us detach from negative emotions and elevates our state of mind, allowing us to rise above anger, resentment, and pride. Suddenly, the world appears more beautiful, and everything begins to feel meaningful and good.

Actionables

Who are the people who have favoured you, from the beginning until now? Reflect on each one and express your sincere thanks, even years later to everyone who has positively impacted your life. Consider the following:

- Family: Mother, Father and/ or Sibling(s)
- Educators: Primary and Secondary School Teachers, College Professors, etc.
- Friends: Old friends
- Everyday heroes: Domestic help, Newspaper delivery person, Milkman, or any other help
- Additional figures: Community members etc.

Reminders:

- Negative emotions disrupt our peace. To make life happy, we need to change ourselves by removing and separating our negative traits.
- Our ego hinders our understanding of others, causing us to overlook their importance.
- Gratitude helps us detach from negative emotions, elevating us above anger and transforming us internally.

SELF-ANALYSIS: AN IDEAL SOLUTION FOR PROBLEMS

TO ACHIEVE HAPPINESS IN LIFE, WE MUST CHANGE OUR perspective. By focusing on our thoughts and viewpoint, everything begins to look different, regardless of external circumstances. Trying to change the world or people around us is an endless and often impossible task, as we have minimal control over our surroundings—whether it be family, relatives, work, or society. Instead of looking outward for happiness and expecting others to change, we should focus on changing ourselves. By understanding this, we develop a more organised way of thinking and more easily achieve our desires.

Our efforts and hard work often go in the wrong direction, and this happens to many people. We frequently blame others, complain that they do not listen or follow us, and express frustration that they go their own way—

trying to impose their will on us. Many people have such complaints. Up until now, you may have worked hard to change others, believing that if your daughter, son, or husband's nature changed, happiness would come into your life. This mindset keeps you worried, always hoping for a change that never comes. How many people have this attitude? How many years have you spent, holding onto this belief? What have you achieved from it? Did you get what you wanted? No. Then why haven't you considered that maybe, the path itself is wrong? The path you have followed and believed to be right might have a flaw. Why hasn't anyone thought about this?

You often explain things to others but sometimes need to understand yourself. Have you ever thought about this perspective? Why does it happen? We all want to be happy and free from worries. You seek practical solutions for a carefree life, but how often do we think about ourselves? When we say to think about ourselves, what does it mean? Is it about family, fitness, or something more? When planning your day, how much time do you allocate for yourself? You plan for work, meetings, kids, groceries, and meals, but how much time do you reserve just for yourself?

To achieve happiness, we first need to identify the root cause of our unhappiness. It is crucial to evaluate—whether the issue stems from others or our own perspective. Problems often arise from our attitudes rather than external circumstances, colleagues, or family members. Just like in medical science, where diagnosis is more crucial than treatment, understanding the root cause is essential, as without accurate diagnosis, treatment cannot begin.

Similarly, to find happiness, we need to analyse ourselves and determine—whether our unhappiness stems from others, or our own shortcomings. Are our worries caused by others, or by our own thinking? Are our problems due to external factors, or our own attitudes? Why not think about yourself? Most people spend little time reflecting on their own thoughts, instead focusing on others. We may think we are doing things for ourselves, but are we truly acting for our own benefit or that of others? When we think that someone else is causing us pain and worry, it is important to understand that the root cause might be our own mindset. How many people truly reflect on themselves? The beginning should be from within.

If an egg is broken by an external force, its life ends. However, when the living being inside the egg breaks through the shell on its own, a new life begins. Growth and progress always come from internal forces, not external ones. Similarly, for a beautiful, happy life, we must rely on internal change, rather than waiting for external influences. We need to wait for internal forces. A good beginning always starts from within and moves outward, not the other way around.

Have you ever seen a seed? When it is planted in the earth, it breaks through the soil and emerges. It starts to sprout, grows into a plant, and eventually becomes a tree. Consider how much adversity the seed overcomes to reach the surface. It faces the weight of the soil and numerous obstacles. Despite having little strength, it pushes through against all odds. Its journey from a seed to a tree, is not from outside to inside but from inside to outside. It endures various conditions like heat, water, wind, storms, and interactions with animals. Despite all these challenges, it grows from a small seed into a large tree, completing its journey. In contrast, humans often try to change external factors in their lives. Many people think that if their family members, colleagues, office environment, and society improves, their life will be filled with happiness. They focus on changing external surroundings rather than the internal growth that matters and makes an actual difference.

A seed and an egg—which struggle from within to achieve their potential—can succeed and fulfil their purpose in life. However, humans—despite having resources and power—often try to change the external world to find happiness. Even with power and money, if we focus on altering the external world, rather than transforming ourselves from within, we may not achieve true happiness.

When addressing your concerns, do you focus on external or internal factors? Is your approach oriented towards external solutions or internal changes? The true resolution begins from within. Altering your perspective and mindset is crucial; the world around you will not change until you do. With a changed viewpoint, everything appears more positive, while an unchanged perspective can make things seem problematic and distressing.

The solution lies in changing your thinking. By shifting your perspective, you will see opportunities where there were once problems. Every question has an answer, and every problem has a solution. Often, we do not search thoroughly, and focus on external issues—neglecting that our perspective might be the real problem. When you look inward, solutions naturally start to appear. The best approach is to introspect and examine your own thoughts and viewpoints. Shifting your perspective can transform your understanding, and resolve many issues. Sometimes, stepping back from the external environment is necessary—to truly see yourself and make meaningful changes.

Inside our bodies, we have a soul with its own voice. To hear it, block out external noises by covering your ears. Focus on the inner sound, similar to the Om chanted during meditation. We often miss this inner sound, because we are distracted by the noise of the external stimuli. Observe your body's automatic functions, like digestion, heartbeat, and blinking—how many of these processes are under conscious control? The greatest wonder in the world is the human body of a living being. It is a unique machine that no one can create, and it works continuously—from the womb to the tomb, automatically.

Similarly, many things in the world work on their own. We need to view life in such a way, that we understand whether the world is making mistakes or we are. Is the problem outside or inside us? Where is the problem? Once we learn to look within and practice self-analysis, we can learn a lot about the world. Those who have not learned this, who have not practiced it—have achieved nothing so far. They will always remain troubled and unhappy, because they have not understood the root cause. Most people do not grasp this, and do not think that the fault lies in their own perspective. Once we start trying to look at it this way, we find that the answer to the question is hidden within the question itself, and solutions to our problems come to us naturally.

Most problems are temporary and solutions come in time. For example, losing a job can be an opportunity for someone to start a business. Instead of worrying, perhaps view it as a chance for a fresh start. Many worries are not real, or they resolve themselves eventually. Time often brings solutions, so focus on calmly planning and analysing your situation.

Self-reflection and introspection are both crucial for maintaining happiness. While introspection focuses on analysing our internal emotional states and motivations at a deeper, often more psychological level, self-reflection leans toward a more deliberate evaluation of our actions and their alignment with our values. Despite these nuances, they share a common purpose: to help us realise that happiness is rooted more in our internal responses than in external events. Through this inward-focus, we move away from blaming circumstances and instead recognise our power in shaping our emotional experiences. By engaging in both practices—introspecting to understand why we feel a certain way, and reflecting on how we respond—we can align our actions with our core values and cultivate a more stable, authentic sense of happiness.

Actionables

- Use the flowchart for solving any problem:

  Do you have any problems in your life?
  - **No**: There is no need to worry.
  - **Yes**:
    - Do you have a solution?
      - **Yes**: No need to worry; you have the solution.
      - **No**: No need to worry; you do not have the solution.
    - **If you are still worried and cannot find a solution**, seek help from an expert, mentor, or wise person. Simply worrying will not resolve the issue but will increase the triggers causing stress and tension.
- Write down your worries and problems, including those related to your family, your work, your society, and any other concerns.
- Identify which of these activities are under your control and which are not.
- Focus on taking action where you have control, and seek solutions or assistance for areas beyond your control.

Reminders:

- Every question has an answer, and every problem has a solution.
- The most effective solutions come from within, not from external sources.
- Through self-analysis, many problems can be resolved more quickly.

THE JOY OF LEAVING IS GREATER THAN THE JOY OF LOSING

We all try to fill our lives with happiness, we try to change our mindset, and we make efforts to understand numerous things. However, the results we expect, often do not turn out the way they should. Where do we go wrong? Perhaps we should learn from those, who have genuinely attained happiness and success—not just in material terms, but in their inner being. The issue arises when we follow individuals, whose actions do not align with their words leading to a loss of trust. Authenticity comes from actions, as true greatness is demonstrated through deeds rather than self-declaration. Great leaders often convey wisdom through their actions, leaving a lasting impact. We should embrace their teachings wholeheartedly.

While many focus solely on personal happiness, those who align their growth with the upliftment of others achieve genuine advancement. Have you ever experienced the joy of giving? There is a deep sense of fulfilment in giving, far greater than in simply receiving. When we give, it may appear as if we are losing something but in reality, we gain far more. Despite what some may think, selfless individuals often benefit the most, their contributions extend well beyond material rewards. We elevate ourselves by bringing happiness to others, spreading joy, and uplifting those around us. If we believe in this, we will surely rise higher. Many find it difficult to grasp this concept, as giving requires a part of ourselves. When it is time to give, attachments and ego often resist, fearing that something personal will be lost. But the truth is clear: if you want to lift yourself, start by lifting someone else.

The concept of परस्परोपग्रहो जीवानाम् *(Parasparopagraho Jivanam)* or mutual benefit was demonstrated by Lord Mahavira, who lived and experienced it himself before sharing this teaching with us. When we share joy with others, we find joy ourselves. When we give happiness to others, we become filled with happiness. Whatever we give to others comes back to us multiplied. This concept appears and extends as a part of various cultural sayings and proverbs, with a common representation also being the idea, that 'happiness shared is happiness doubled.'

We often find ourselves fixated on what is immediate and tangible, driven by a fear of losing something. When we act for others, there is a common concern that we are sacrificing something of our own—as if we are losing or giving away too much. Yet, in selfless giving, we often discover that we receive much more in return, uplifting ourselves in the process. However, according to Lord Mahavira, true altruism may not be possible. Every act of giving, whether to objects or individuals, inevitably carries some element of self-interest. Grasping this concept is essential, as many people live their lives misguidedly due to a lack of proper understanding of this principle.

When we interact with any non-living objects, the way we handle them affects their performance. If you use a pen roughly, for instance, it will not last as long. Similarly, if you have a car, the better care you take of it, the longer it will serve you. Even though a car has no emotions or feelings, it performs better when treated well.

Take any living being and observe: the better care and treatment you provide, the more it returns to you. For example, look at a cow. If you provide it with a little care, it will give you so much in return throughout its life. A cow gives back not only during its lifetime, but even after it passes away. You feed and care for the cow, and in return, it provides you with milk, curd, ghee, and even medicinal benefits from its urine and dung. It helps in curing ailments and provides various forms of support. Even though it might seem like you are doing a favour to the cow, in reality, you are benefiting from it in numerous ways. You might feel like you are giving a lot, but you are essentially doing it for your own benefit. The cow serves as an instrument for your benefit, and understanding this can reveal the true nature of giving and receiving.

Consider a seed: if you provide it with a bit of care, remove its hard shell, and create the right environment with fertile soil, you will eventually receive much more in return. The seed appears small and insignificant, but it has the potential to yield countless seeds in the future. Initially, you may think you are doing a lot for the seed, but in reality, you are only providing the necessary conditions for its growth. The seed, once it grows into a tree and bears fruit, repays your effort manifold. While your effort is short-term, the benefits continue for years. The tree provides fruit, flowers, fragrance, shade, cooling, fresh oxygen, a safe environment, and beauty. So, even though it may seem like you are giving and providing for the sake of the seed, what you receive in return is far greater than what you initially gave.

When you offer a smile, kind words, or comforting and empathetic support to someone, what happens to the atmosphere around you? We are not even talking about money here. Just offering a few soothing words or empathy can transform the environment. The person you support becomes profoundly connected to you. When you extend your shoulder for support or lend a helping hand, they may become deeply grateful and regard you with reverence. You might feel that you are giving to them, but in reality, the act of giving fills you with joy. This process leads to physical, psychological, and financial changes. The environment around you shifts positively, as well. By adopting a giving attitude, you naturally fill yourself with positivity and humbleness.

Medical science indicates, that the secretion of certain enzymes can have significant health benefits. These enzymes can greatly strengthen our mental state and elevate our mood. For example, when you forgive someone, the joy and peace you experience from forgiveness are profound. You are not just giving forgiveness; you are receiving it in return. Forgiveness brings a sense of relief and joy, unlike the anger and bitterness that can arise from holding grudges. In essence, you are the one gaining from the act of giving forgiveness. This principle is reflected in the idea of upliftment of others, where the true benefit lies in the self.

We all must let go of certain things in life. When a person willingly chooses to let go, they find true contentment. However, if letting go happens involuntarily or out of necessity, it can lead to a feeling of loss or distress. True happiness comes from voluntary self-sacrifice; when you willingly let go, you find joy. The joy of giving is distinct from the discomfort of forced release. Craving accumulation releases dopamine, leading to further cravings and illness, while giving releases oxytocin, bringing love and happiness. When you give selflessly—whether a smile, kind words, or support—it creates bonds and brings affection in return.

Many expect love and care from others but feel neglected when it is not received, often because their desire to give is tied to receiving something in return. Genuine love and care come from selfless giving, not expecting anything back. If giving is conditional, it becomes a transaction rather than an act of true generosity. Life reflects what you give, and so, selfless actions always return multiplied. This principle applies to all relationships, including those with partners, children, friends, and even in interactions with non-living things. True generosity involves giving without hidden self-interest or expectations.

If we offer love and care selflessly—even just a smile or a few kind words—we create a world where everything we give comes back to us many times over. The principle is simple: the only condition is that it should be selfless. Whether it is about charity or any act of giving, do so with a selfless attitude. This will become your virtue. You will find happiness in giving, and this happiness is not just a matter of the future or the next life; it will manifest immediately in this life—physically, mentally, and in every way possible. You will notice changes in all aspects of your life. This is the essence of the joy of giving. When someone gives with a truly selfless mindset—whether it is a small gesture, a smile, a kind word, a helping hand, or offering their heart and support—the entire world seems to become their own. Assisting someone, especially those in need, often returns to them in kind—creating a cycle of positivity and fulfilment.

Let's focus on a small incident: There was a poor boy who only lived with his elderly mother. He was in tenth grade and managed both his studies and his household, by selling small items door-to-door after school. One hot day, exhausted and hungry, he decided to ask for food at the next house. As the poor boy knocked on the door for food, a kind girl offered him a glass of milk without hesitation. Years later, the boy became a doctor. When the girl, now a woman in need, came to his hospital, he recognised her and covered her medical bill, reminding her that she had already paid it, years ago with her kindness. This story is a prime example of how the girl's selfless act, had returned to her in her time of need.

When we give, we often do so with hidden selfish motives, even in our closest relationships. True selfless giving should come from genuine compassion, not from any obligation or expectation. Recognising and letting go of selfish motives allows us to give freely and joyfully to others. Authentic generosity, which is not influenced by external pressures, enriches both the giver and the receiver. In neurotherapy, positive thoughts and inner happiness promote healing—by activating the body's natural enzymes. Compassion and gratitude balance our aura and enhance our well-being, while negative emotions like selfishness cloud it. Dharma teaches us that selflessness leads to a positive and healthy state of mind.

Lord Mahavira's teachings emphasise the profound impact of selfless giving—whether through financial support, acts of service, kind words, or simple gestures of comfort. By giving without expecting anything in return, we enhance our own physical and mental well-being, while nurturing a positive environment around us. The joy derived from selfless acts, extends beyond material contributions—with even a genuine smile or encouraging words having the power to uplift others. Lord Mahavira's principle of mutual support for living beings illustrates that in aiding others, we ultimately enrich our own lives. Embracing this mindset, nurtures a cycle of positivity and well-being; creating a harmonious atmosphere for everyone involved.

Actionables

- Reflect on the difference between giving with genuine happiness, versus giving with a sense of entitlement or a desire to show off. How does each approach affect the recipient and your own experience?
- Identify someone in your life—or in the wider world—to whom you truly give selflessly. Consider instances where you have offered something, with no expectation of receiving anything in return.
- Examine whether you view yourself as the primary beneficiary when helping others, or if you see the recipient as the true beneficiary of your actions.

Reminders:

- We cannot truly give something to anyone, because every act of giving carries some element of self-interest—whether we are dealing with objects or living beings.
- When a person willingly chooses to let go, they find true contentment. However, if letting go happens involuntarily or out of necessity, it can lead to a feeling of loss or distress.
- True happiness comes from voluntary self-sacrifice; when you willingly let go, you find joy.
- The joy of giving and the satisfaction it brings are distinct from the discomfort of having to release something unwillingly.

REAL HAPPINESS IS NEVER
FOUND OUTSIDE OF US;
IT LIES WITHIN US.

ACKNOWLEDGEMENTS

I extend my heartfelt gratitude to Niryapak Muni Shree Veer Sagar Ji Maharaj for his profound wisdom and guidance. He has been an unwavering source of inspiration.

My deepest gratitude goes to Sant Shiromani Acharya Shree Vidya Sagar Ji Maharaj for his divine influence. I offer my heartfelt gratitude and reverence to Acharya Shree Samay Sagar Ji Maharaj for his blessings and spiritual inspiration. I also extend my humble gratitude to Muni Shree Vishal Sagar Ji, Muni Shree Dhaval Sagar Ji, Muni Shree Utkrisht Sagar Ji, and all the Kshullak Ji in the Muni Sangh for their continued blessings.

Thanks to the entire Gurubhakt Pariwar for their unwavering support and spiritual strength.

A special appreciation goes to Ashish Tholiya for reviewing the manuscript and providing valuable feedback.

Heartfelt thanks to Jyash Tholiya, a child prodigy known for memorising and singing the national anthems of all UNrecognised countries of the world. His encouragement was vital throughout this process.

I extend my heartfelt thanks to Sanjeev Jain (New Delhi) and Ankit Jain (Agra) for their exceptional ideas for the cover page design.

I would like to express my sincere gratitude to Wasim Helal for the beautiful cover design. I would also like to extend heartfelt thanks to my publisher at AMARYLLIS, Vikas Rakheja, and managing editor Bidisha Srivastava, for their unwavering belief in me and *The Quest for Happiness*. Trisha, thank you for your editorial inputs on the book.

TRACING THE SPIRITUAL JOURNEY

Acharya Shree Vidya Sagar Ji

Navacharya Shree Samay Sagar Ji

Niryapak Muni Shree Veer Sagar Ji

Born as Shailesh Jain, Niryapak Muni Shree Veer Sagar Ji has dedicated his entire life to attaining spirituality and pursuing the Jain path of liberation. Belonging to a devout Jain family, he grew up in a nurturing environment where values were given importance. Despite having a strong blend of academic commitment and diverse professional experience, he always felt inclined towards higher spiritual ideals and self-discipline.

Shailesh Ji managed his own business until he took on a three-year Brahmacharya vow (remaining celibate) marking a deeper spiritual commitment. Following that, he accepted the Aajivan Brahmacharya Vrat, and ultimately received his Muni Diksha (initiation) from Acharya Shree Vidya Sagar Ji Maharaj, and was spiritually nurtured and mentored by Acharya Shree Samay Sagar Ji. His life story exemplifies the power of resilience, purpose, inner transformation, and embracing a life devoted to a higher divine calling.

ABOUT THE WRITER

Dr Jyoti Jain Tholiya is an Associate Professor of Architecture in Pune, with over twenty years of academic and professional experience across countries. *The Quest for Happiness* is a tribute to Niryapak Muni Shree Veer Sagar Ji and explores how individuals worldwide can seek perpetual fulfilment, rooted in self-awareness and emotional well-being.